MALI WORKHOUSE

1719 - 1875

AN
ARCHITECTURAL
HISTORY
1719-1997

PEGGY EDMOND

Published by M. Edmond 1999

St. Clare's Hospice

ISBN 0 9536147 0 0

Printed and bound in Great Britain
by Blackwater Printing
Heybridge, Maldon.

Proceeds donated to St Clare's Hospice,
Heybridge, Maldon.

A
Thomas Plume
1630-1704
Archdeacon of Rochester

"...... I also give what remains of my personal estate in the Exchequer towards erecting a workhouse for the poor of Maldon and the surrounding villages......"

(from a copy of his will, 1719)
By Kind permission of the Plume Trustees.

Preface

This booklet is the outcome of a unique set of circumstances in that the author, a trained historian, lived for nearly fifty years in part of the building being researched. Over these years it was possible to accumulate the, very, few and fragmentary documentary references and to record at random intervals the physical details as they became relevant or before they disappeared forever.

The early chapters, therefore, are a narrative of the way in which this was done until sufficient 'layers' had been peeled off to reveal the original building. The later chapters, in chronological order, outline the architectural history at four stages: i.e. 1719 - 1835 when it was, firstly, a single, two-storey block known as Maldon Workhouse, serving the three parishes of Maldon All Saints, St Peter's and St Mary's; and run by the officers of the Parish Councils. Around 1750 a back, Western, block was added and at the turn of the century it was housing, approximately 50 inmates and a 100 plus occasional (casual). From 1835 - 1873 it was known as the Union Workhouse having been enlarged up to a capacity of 350, to receive the poor from the 3 Maldon parishes and 29 others on either side of the Blackwater estuary. This building was administered by a Board of Guardians. After the new workhouse was built on a green field site in Spital Road (now St Peter's Hospital) , the old building, still referred to as 'The Spike' for many years, was sold on the open market and later renamed Nos. 1 - 5/6 Hillside.

In order to avoid the frequent, irritating, repetition of the phrase - (see fig...) - - the diagrams have been placed within the text to which they are relevant.

There are a number of standard books on workhouses in general, mainly dealing with administration and finance and/or the social aspects of the life of the inmates. Any of these would provide background information; but nothing dealing solely with the architecture of any other comparable workhouse appears to have been published so a bibliography has not been provided.

There are a few old photographs of Hillside but I am overwhelmingly indebted to the late C. G. Tait for his patience and skill in producing the artist's impressions of the three stages of the workhouse building without which the booklet would be immeasurably poorer.

I wish to thank the Archivist and his staff at the Essex Record Office for their help and permission to incorporate quotes and documents, as indicated in the text; Maldon Town Council and the Plume Trustees for

B
John Sadd c 1823

Superintendent of Building Works

[from The Continuing Years by P K Kemp]
By kind permission of the Maldon Museum

permission to copy the portrait of Thomas Plume and Maldon Museum and the Sadd family for permission to copy the portrait of John Sadd; the staff at the Public Record Office and the Norwich Union Insurance Company for their, albeit negative, searches; The Ordnance Survey for permission to use the map of central Maldon and John Prime for permission to use the modern photograph; and the, then, owners of Nos. 1, 2 and 4 Hillside and the present owner of No. 3, for permission to take photographs of their property.

My thanks are also due to Ian Edmond for photography and tracing plans; Paul Sharp for photography and computer editing and graphics; Jerry Edmond for photography and Joe Brannigan for making a video. Finally I wish to thank Dr William Petchey for his invaluable advice and encouragement.

FOR

JERRY and SUE and COLIN

Peggy Edmond
Maldon
1999

Contents

N.B. Old-style units of money and measurement have been used to preserve authenticity.

Introduction

We bought 3, Hillside, Market Hill, Maldon in April 1948. At that time, just after the end of the Second World War, it was nearly impossible to find somewhere to live, either rented or bought. The housing stock had been badly depleted by bombing raids and all were badly dilapidated. Large numbers of service men were wanting their own homes and many more, younger, people were marrying now that the war was over. An effort at fairness was made by the allocation of 'Housing Points' to couples on council waiting lists: long time residence and education in the area qualified for more points; as did wartime service, the number of children, chronic disease and present over-crowding. The waiting list was very long and, where possible, people tried to find their own accommodation, though this was very difficult with a small baby.

The property was advertised as ... Freehold terrace: 7 rooms and all main services ...for £750 with some furniture to remain. It comprised, on three floors, ... living room, sitting room and scullery; three rooms; two large rooms; and underground cellar. Before we bought it the vendor was required to paint it internally as it was so filthy, but it had no wood-worm and no rats. He did paint it - everything - with a thin coat of dull, coffee-coloured whitewash sprayed all over everything, including the lavatory seat and the door knobs. We paid, eventually, £700 and moved in at Easter. We sub-let the top floor, which was self-contained by reason of a double door half way up the top flight of stairs, to another young couple giving them carte blanche to modernise and decorate as they wished.

This left us to modernise and repair two floors and the cellar, which we immediately discovered was not 'underground' but has a 7′ 6″ ceiling height and a full-sized door giving access to the back garden. This was because of the slope of Market Hill and resulted in the property being three storeys at the front and four at the back. The first requirement was to turn one of the three rooms on the middle floor into a bathroom although this would leave us with only two rooms for use as bedrooms, and a very large bathroom. The scullery had to be up-graded to a kitchen; the whole house rewired for electricity; gas and a hot water system laid on since the "mains services" as advertised consisted of one electric light and four gas rings, all in the back living room.

These improvements cost us a further £150 and at times proved less straightforward than we, or the workman, expected: as, for instance, when the gas fitter broke three heavy duty chisels trying to cut a groove for the supply pipe across a 9″ oak beam. The major, initial, repair work was to salvage the front bay windows the woodwork of which, especially on the middle floor, was rotten and the glass falling out. This necessitated lowering a 4"x4" sill of new timber on a block and tackle from the floor above and rebuilding several of the window frames.

We were soon made aware that older Maldonians referred to the building as the "Spike". In Dickensian lore all workhouses had spikes on top of the walls to deter the inmates from climbing out and this became vernacular shorthand amongst local people. This usage was our first intimation that what we had bought was, indeed, part of a workhouse. We were also told that Cromwell Lane had been known as Union Lane during the 19th Century and as we began to look round and study the construction of the building it became obvious that it had been a large complex of rooms and outbuildings. The seven rooms, as advertised, proved to be a basic six, two on each floor, plus the cellar. All were very large: those at the front being a basic 17′ 6″ x 21′ into a 3′ bay; those at the back: 22′ x 22′ but divided on each floor into smaller units, creating a 6′ x 6′ kitchen and a 6′ x 8′ "office" on the "ground" floor; a 14′ 6″ x 9′ bedroom, sacrificed to make a bathroom, on the middle floor and a second kitchen, 11′ 6″ x 10′ 6″, on the top floor. The rooms on the middle and top floor front were narrower on account of a 3′ 9″ landing and a 3′ 3″ boxed insertion for the stair-well of No 4. This resulted in a peculiar alcove in both rooms which was even odder since the fireplaces in these rooms were in the corner thus created. All the front rooms had this a-symmetrical corner position for the fireplace occasioned by the need to make use of the existing chimney-breast, three-quarters being in No 3 and the remaining portion providing the fireplace for No 4. All, in No. 3, had Victorian cast-iron basket grates, and we had to be given right of way for our smoke to go up the chimney of No. 4.

Every room in the property had other quirks and anomalies the full significance of many of which did not become apparent until detailed research was undertaken.

HILLSIDE, MARKET HILL

EAST FRONT (LOOKING NORTH)

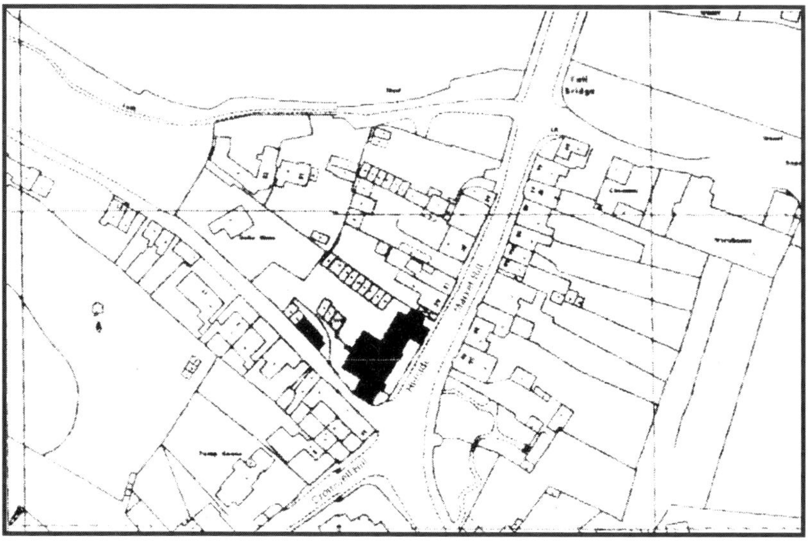

SITE MAP ©Crown copyright, MC99/349

TELEPHONE
CHELMSFORD 2380
IPSWICH 2795

Established 40 years.

TELEGRAMS
COBBE WINCER, CHELMSFORD
COBBE WINCER, IPSWICH

COBBE & WINCER

Partners: S. G. Wincer and A. Wincer

Auctioneers, Land & Estate Agents, Valuers

3 DUKE STREET, CHELMSFORD

And at 7, ARCADE STREET, IPSWICH

SPECIALISTS IN COUNTRY HOUSES AND FARMS THROUGHOUT EAST ANGLIA

TO:- R.McDonald, Esq., BY APPOINTMENT.

PLEASE PERMIT BEARER TO VIEW:-

No.2, HILLSIDE,
M A L D O N,
E S S E X.

FOR IMMEDIATE SALE WITH POSSESSION. OWNER GOING ABROAD.

A FREEHOLD TERRACE HOUSE CONTAINING SEVEN ROOMS WITH ALL MAIN SERVICES CONNECTED. BACK YARD. VACANT POSSESSION. FREEHOLD £750 INCLUDING SOME FURNITURE.

MALDON, ESSEX:- Situate about 2 minutes walk from the High Street with Shops etc., and about 5 minutes walk from station, 10 miles from Chelmsford, 12 miles by road from Burnham-on-Crouch and 44 miles from London by road.

BUS SERVICES to all parts.

THIS FREEHOLD TERRACE HOUSE

built of brick, lath and plaster and containing:-

On the Ground Floor:- LIVING ROOM, SITTING ROOM and Scullery.
On the First Floor:- THREE ROOMS.
On the Top Floor:- TWO LARGE ROOMS.

Underground cellar.

The front room on each floor has a large bay window.

N.B. The house needs redecorating throughout and this is now being carried out by the Owner and will be included in the sale.

ALL MAIN SERVICES CONNECTED.

Back Yard.

RATES amount to about £3.5.0d a year. Water Rate 15/-d a year.

[illegible]

PRICE FREEHOLD £750 (SEVEN HUNDRED & FIFTY POUNDS) FOR QUICK SALE, including some furniture.

Chapter 1
Hillside in 1948

This description of the property, as bought in 1948, uses the past tense occasionally to draw attention to those features which no longer exist or have been significantly altered over the past fifty years.

The principal feature noticeable on first entering the ground floor front room is the massive beam: an 8″ cube 21′ 0″ in length fixed at either end into 10 $^1/_2$″ cube posts 7′ 6″ high which continue upwards into the room above, where the beam is anchored by grown timber knees 3′ 0″ on each arm fastened by tren-nails. This, front room, beam is reinforced along its entire length by 7″ x 6″ cut timber, with straight knees, fixed by iron bars at either end and six 3″ bolts. A similar beam, not reinforced, forms the ceiling edge on the South side of the room but there is no beam on the North side. The South wall is well- made, tongued and grooved pine panelling forming part of the stair- well. On the East a cross beam frames the, almost, floor length bay window, while the front door and half a window account for the rest. This half window, of which the remainder is in the communal passage, thereby giving the appearance of a complete window from the outside, is set behind a post with its sill cut round the post. The lower two thirds of the West, or fireplace, wall is roughly assembled 9″ pine planking with plaster above, and has a cross beam anchored into the brickwork of the chimney-breast. Only one full cross joint, and one half length, is visible: both "disappearing" into No. 4; there being therefore, disappointingly, no fully beamed ceiling. There are two steps up to the house door and the floor level of the other rooms. The house door is a double thickness plank door, vertical on the room side and horizontal on the other, with two heavy iron bar hinges and a wrought iron latch.

Opposite the house door is a similarly constructed door giving access to the communal passage along which we had right of way. Between these two doors is the front staircase. This is strikingly unusual in being 3′ 9″ wide, with 6″ risers x 10″ treads and 15 steps in all. Immediately at the top is a small cubicle for the W.C. This is well constructed of double skinned, tongued and grooved 4″ pine planks but has only one very small window giving direct light and air although there are two further, internal, windows of little practical use. The whole cubicle is anchored to another post with grown knees and contained a high-level cistern with chain link pull.

The house wall of the middle front room consists of another double-skinned partition: tongued and grooved vertically on the landing side with alternately proud vertical planks on the other. Painted black and white this gives a superficial appearance of half timbering. This partition is propped on a skirting board of varying depth, to take account of the inward slope of the floor, and contained two doors.

HILLSIDE, MARKET HILL
No.3 Internal - 1948

W

as bought
Freehold terrace
7 rooms all
main services
£750 to include
some furniture

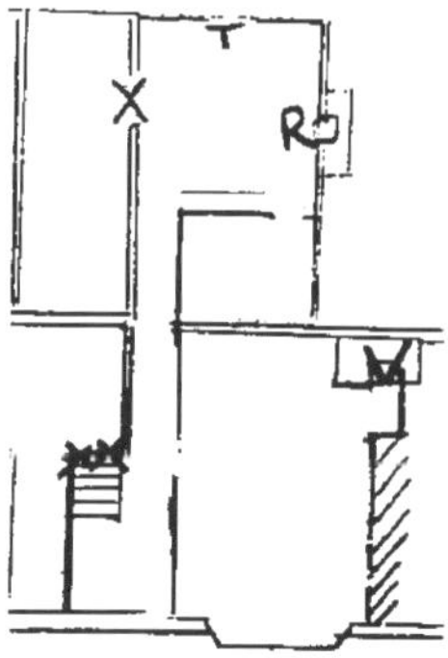

X	blocked doors
XX	front door half-way upstairs
V	cast-iron gates
R	ranges
T	cold water taps
//////	stairwell for No.4 cheap partition
E	one, naked lightbulb
M	four penny-in-the-slot gas meters
C	coal cellars
A	Half winbdow in passage
↑ (dashed arrow)	Right of way along communal passage
B	Back stairs up Cellar stairs down
0	Doric pillar

2 large rooms (sic)
SECOND FLOOR (TOP) FLOOR

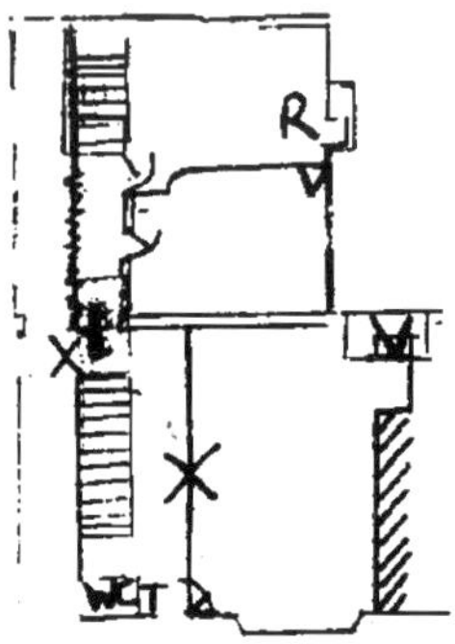

3 rooms
FIRST (MIDDLE) FLOOR

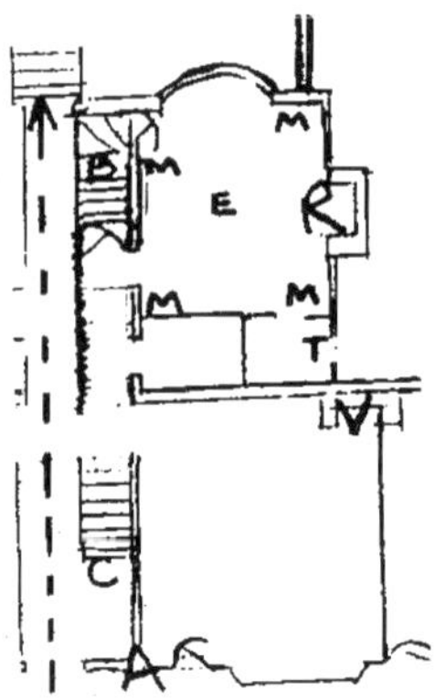

Living room
Sitting room
Scullery

GROUND FLOOR

MARKET HILL

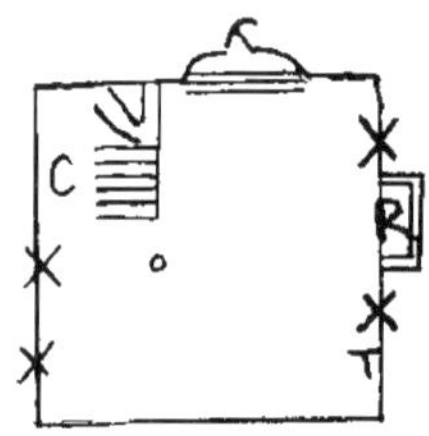

LOWER
GROUND FLOOR
(CELLAR)
Underground (sic)

One, in the corner nearest the head of the stairs and the lavatory, was flimsy and shoddily made; the other had been removed leaving only the casing filled by three wider planks than those used in the partition. As well as the off-centre fireplace, the stair well box for next door creates an alcove. There was also, alarmingly, a gap between the main and cross beam, out of which, from time to time, pieces of inserted packing fell.

The top flight of stairs, apart from the double doors half way up, is of the same proportions as the middle flight but the top front room has a less heavy beam structure and only one, central, door. There are, however, two boarded up trap doors and another on the landing which gives access to a lead-roofed catwalk between the two basic blocks, front and back, of the whole building.

The back block, based on the 22′ 0″ x 22′ 0″ area on each floor, is only relevant to Nos. 2 and 3, Nos. 1, 4 and 5 not extending so far. It is, therefore, possible to have windows on the North wall which enabled the main areas to be divided, in varying proportions. The windows in this block are sash as opposed to those in the front, except the bays, which are casement.

The beam and deep coved ceiling of the top floor room are repeated in the back, as is the half-boarding and plaster to the walls. The entrance door is very heavy duty, more like an external quality although the door into the "kitchen", cut into a flimsy edge on edge partition, is mean and shoddy. A door which would have given access to No. 2 had merely been nailed up. There is yet another trapdoor and the fireplace contained a kitchen range although the mantelpiece is a graceful cast-iron feature with pilasters, swags and urns as decoration.

At the bottom of the top flight of stairs is another door giving access to No. 2, again battened and nailed up. The wall along the back landing between No. 2 and 3 is of the cheaper edge to edge construction with 4″x4″ posts and planks presenting a mock beam effect. This back hall and the stairs leading down to the first floor are not the public width of the front flights, being only 3′ 0″ wide with 6″ risers and 13 x 12″ treads. The cheap partition ends at the 6th step (down) after which the better quality tongued and grooved planking forms a cupboard stair-well with a door giving access to the ground floor. The 13th step of the flight is on the room side of the door which has two small glass panels to light the stair well. Under the cheap partition there are slots for previous banisters.

The two rooms leading off the back landing together make up the basic 22′ 0″ x 22′ 0″ area but were divided when built. The smaller, with a North window, had to be sacrificed to make a bathroom. The glaring anomaly in this room is a curved wall with a very narrow Victorian fireplace set across the far corner;

the concave side of this wall is in the next room, the entrance door of which is immediately at the top of the stairs leaving no room to manoeuvre when it became necessary to place a chimney flue in the external stack which already existed: hence the oddity of the wall. Both rooms have sash windows but that in the bathroom has 1 six-pane light and 1 three-pane upper light whereas the back room has 2 six-pane lights, in the West wall. Both doors are four-panelled and have now got brass handles although only those in the bathroom are original. Like the main room above, the back room had a kitchen range; it also has a walk in cupboard over the lower stair-well.

The "ground" floor back had also been subdivided when built giving, as the main room, 14′ 6″ x 15′ 6″ with a small 6′ 0″ x 6′ 0″ scullery lit by another nine-pane sash window. The principal architectural feature of this room is a 7′ 0″ bow window on the West wall. This is 20″ deep and consists of three 5′ 6″ lights divided by 2′ 6″ wide verticals. The centre light has upper and lower sections of three 2-pane; the outer two have similar but only 2 x 2; all are sash. This window is set within a 27″ deep x 8′ 0″ wide x 7′ 9″ casing rising to 8′ 6″ behind a 9″ dropped ceiling. It had 3 panes of original glass: now, alas broken. The walls are half-board and plaster above and the doors well built, 4- panel with cheap brass knobs, subsequently replaced by reproduction Georgian handles. The fireplace contained a range and this was the room with the only gas and electricity "as advertised".

The "scullery" had one cold tap and a shallow yellowstone sink. It also has good quality pine shelving forming a work top with (missing) drawers underneath, which continued into the "office" where part of the shelving, at eye level, is two cupboards with keyholes. The door to the office opens outwards and has only a keyhole: no handle or knob at all. The back hall has the same partition with mock beam effect as the back landing except that one section opposite the room door had a three-paned window to afford some light at the top of the cellar stairs.

The stairs / steps to the cellar are 3′ 0″ wide and the flight consists of 7 wooden and 4 stone slab on brick with ten 5″ treads and 7″ risers. The wooden steps may also be on brick as they have 8″ treads with a $2^1/_2$″ addition and the wooden risers prevent the bricks being seen. The whole area is 22′ 0″ x 21′ 6″ as the South wall runs under, and supports, the central passage of the whole block. Extra support is also provided by an octagonal, wooden, Doric pillar set in a stone plinth. The garden door, up three stone steps repeats the bow shape of the window in the room above, being flanked by two 4-pane vertical lights. The door itself has a glazed upper quarter but is of a flimsy construction and has a bakelite door knob. The entire construction is cut into a 24″ thick brick wall topped by an 18″ beam and repeats the dropped ceiling effect. The North wall had a blocked door and a window and between them an 11′0″ stone fireplace containing two 3′0″ kitchen ranges. Under the window was a yellowstone sink with one cold tap.

The East wall has full length shelving on iron brackets and the South wall had a further two doors, initially nailed up but now removed and bricked up. The ceiling joists are exposed. The floor is flag-stoned. In the space between the stairs and the South wall: i.e. under the central passage, there is a small narrow, 3′ 0″ x 6′ 0″ compartment separated from the stair well by a line of 1″ x 1″ struts 4″ apart forming the banisters to the stairs but also giving light to the cubicle. The use to which this cubicle was put was not readily apparent but it became the coal cellar after the cupboard under our stairs in the communal passage became needed for bicycles.

The cellar door gives directly onto a flagged footpath which turns, at right angles, to join a communal path over which, again, we have right of way. The garden for No. 3 was long and narrowing toward the West finishing about 35′ 0″ down the path with a 3′ 0″ brick wall and a broken down wicket gate, rarely opened. Looking back, Eastward, from this gate, the most striking feature is the sheer height of the building since one is standing at, lower, ground level and there are four storeys. The problem of building on a site with both a down-ward and back-ward slope had been solved by creating a series of brick boxes such that No. 1 has a 5′ 0″ retaining wall with a short flight of external, stone steps; No. 2 has a half height cellar; No. 3 a full height cellar and Nos. 4, 5 and 6 have a 7′ 6″ retaining wall with no cellar and no steps. Only Nos. 2 and 3, have, in fact, the "back" block of the property. Both Nos. 2 and 3 had bow windows at the first floor level, that of No. 3 having a brick framework for the garden door and windows while that of No. 2 was supported on two 4″ x 4″ posts making a canopy to the entrance door. Between these two, bays, is a 6′ 4″ panelled door at the top of a flight of 9 stone steps leading to the communal passage. This door is set between very plain moulded 7″ pilasters with an equally plain fanlight and tablature. The steps have 10$^1/_2$″ treads and 7″ risers and there is a wrought iron balustrade on either side.

There is no garden wall, or fence, between Nos. 3, 2 or 1 but the boundary wall between the property and Cromwell, late Union, Lane presents several anomalies, on both sides: the most obvious, and interesting, being a nailed up door hung in space on the property side yet at ground level to the lane. This wall commences as modern brick round the front courtyard; it then continues with successively more old brick until it becomes the Southern house wall of No. 1 up to the first floor level and then continues, at that height, down the lane to become the house wall of an outbuilding which is one storey fronting the lane but two inside the property. There are four bricked up windows in the building and the front wall then continued down the lane in varying stages of decay but showing clearly capped posts for entrance gates at two sites before turning North and then East to encompass the whole site. The split-level construction of the outbuilding illustrates, again, the difficulties of the site and the lower level of the surface of the lane pertaining when building took place. To the East of the outbuilding is an entrance door

HILLSIDE, MARKET HILL
No.3 External - 1948

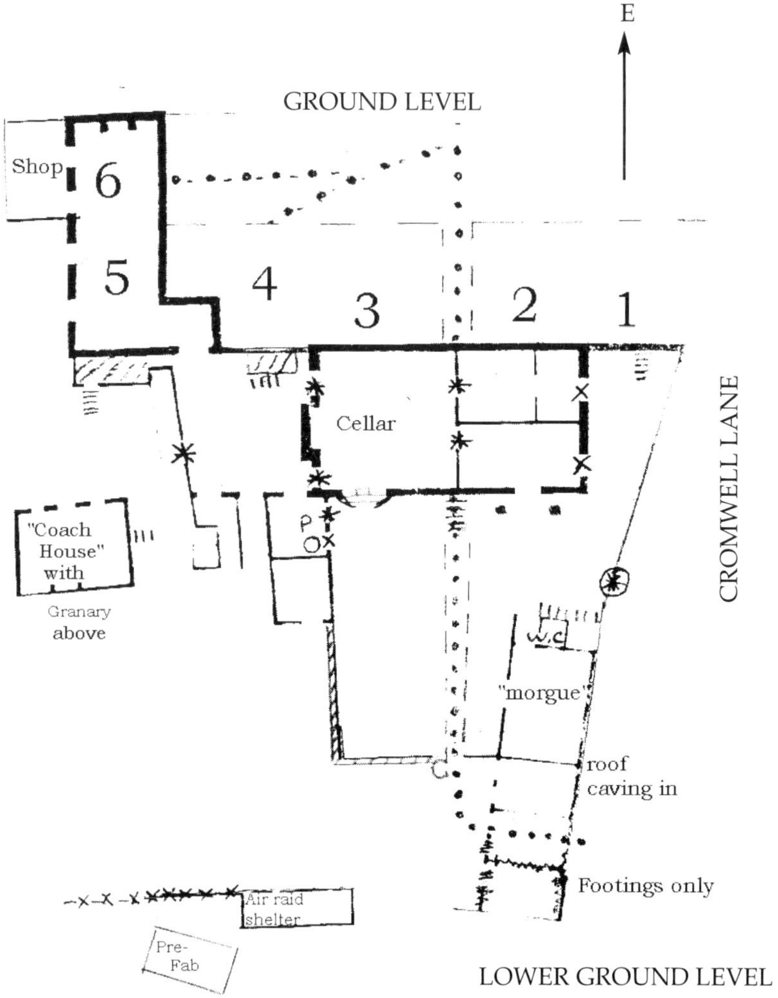

••••	right of way	O	well
•-•-•	right of way	⊛	blocked door (suspended in air)
*	blocked doors	-x-x-	Tudor drain
x	blocked windows	P	Pump
▤	Steps/ladders to lower ground level	XXXXX	Party wall
▭	staging	G	Gate
		o o	Posts

leading to a flight of ten stone steps down to the lower ground level and to the right of them the "hung" door. This led, at the time, to speculation that the outbuilding had been the "morgue" and the useless door the paupers' last exit.

There were garden walls between Nos. 3, 4, 5 and 6; that between 3 and 4 being 7′ 0″ high and having various outbuildings incorporated into it on No. 4's side. It had a blocked-up door and window and, curiously, did not come away from the corner of No. 3 but from about 2′ 0″ nearer the bow window. The individual garden access for Nos. 4 and 5 was at first floor level onto a heavy wooden staging from doors set into window apertures; and then down heavy open-tread ladders. A similar ladder gave access to the upper floor of an outbuilding, referred to locally as the coach house and granary, which was part of No. 5's property.

Although, not visible from No. 3 there was a well and pump in the outbuildings of No. 4. There was also an uninhabited "pre-fab" in the Westernmost part of the grounds, and an air raid shelter.

Chapter 2
Hillside 1948 - 1997

In general it appeared, from the foregoing description, that the property had been built in three stages and altered over a period of nearly 300 years, the exact dating of which has been achieved by painstaking research. To begin with, apart from making the property habitable and keeping it in repair there was neither money for major alterations nor time for research but such work as was carried out began, over the years, to clarify the picture. Since there was no money, very few mistakes were made by destroying features in the early years which subsequently proved integral to the research.

The kitchen ranges, except in the cellar, were thrown out (literally from the windows) and went for scrap. The fireplace in the middle floor back room was bricked up and those in the top and ground floor bricked round a modern grate. The Victorian grates were left in situ, except for that in the top front room; unfortunately in the early 1950's that in the ground-floor front room was replaced by a, then, modern, low-level, tiled surround and hearth. In the early 1960's the top, front, room was incorporated into the main property and the door across the top staircase removed. In the late 1960's when a TV aerial was installed it was discovered that the West wall of the ground floor back room was 2 feet thick. At this time, also, a timber preservation company replaced about a third of the floorboards in the top front room which were infested with furniture beetle but gave a clean bill of health to all the other woodwork. In the early 1970's an entrance lobby and downstairs cloakroom were created in the South-East corner of the ground floor front room; the wall between the kitchen and the office was moved to enlarge the kitchen to 8′ 0″ x 6′ 0″ and in 1977 the Victorian fireplace and mantle shelf from the middle front room was moved downstairs to restore the original feature instead of the tiled "mistake". Other cosmetic and decorative changes were carried out but none did damage to the original features and many finished off rougher and cheaper work. During this time the properties on either side became more dilapidated and no visible alterations, either structural or cosmetic, were made except that a bungalow was built round the shell of the pre-fab. in 1959, at which time also a Tudor brick drain was revealed. Eventually, in 1973, Nos. 2, 4, 5 and 6 were acquired by a small local firm of developers and, it was hoped, very necessary repairs and renovations would take place.

The developers intended to create flats out of Nos. 2, 5 and 6 and a town house out of No. 4. To this end they demolished various features of those parts of the property. The most significant demolitions were the destruction of the shop front of No. 6; the removal of the chimneys on the North and East faces of No. 5; and the staging at the rear of Nos. 5 and 6. The "granary / coach house", party garden walls and chimney in No. 2's front ground-floor room were taken apart and the bricks salvaged. The ceiling of the back ground floor room in No. 2, which had a plaster rose and decorated cornice, was also smashed. The removal of the shop front revealed a coach arch and the two wooden gates folded back to form the North and South walls of the shop. Unfortunately they were too dilapidated to be replaced as gates but the plans allowed for the arch to be refurbished and become a pedestrian right of way. The demolition of the chimneys on the East face of No. 5 resulted in the opening up of the, previously, blind windows on the middle and top floor. The absence of the staging at the rear of No. 4 revealed a lower, ground-level, door with internal steps leading up to their kitchen. The rubble accumulated by broken bricks and footings had to be cleared by a bulldozer which, in spite of repeated warnings, hit the edge of the well and came to an abrupt halt. Work also came to a halt because the expense of making the well secure enough for the projected multiple-occupancy led to negotiations to realign the garden wall of No. 3 so that the well was sited in that property. A lead pipe serving the, demolished, outbuildings was also revealed; this was truncated to discharge running water into the well. Other negotiations led to the surrender of our right of way along the communal passage; and half of our garden to make room for the required number of garages, in return for a garage of our own. The North window in the cellar was altered to make a door giving internal access to this garage: the sink under the window was rebuilt on its own plinth in the corner of the cellar and the cold tap re-routed to serve it.

When the work on turning Nos. 5 and 6 into self-contained flats, one on each floor, (Nos. 5, 6 and 7) and a basement studio apartment (No. 8) was completed, No. 4 was sold to a private buyer. The "morgue" had also been sold, as a separate property with its own boundaries. During all this time we had employed a surveyor to safeguard our interests since it was felt that the integrated nature of the original structure was not fully appreciated. In the event this proved an unnecessary precaution as no new cracks or fault lines occurred even to the extent that a piece of stamp paper used as a tell-tale across the gap between the main and cross joists in the middle front room did not, and has not, split to this present day. No progress was made on modernising No. 2 for several years. Eventually surveyors were sent by Essex County Council to check for structural deterioration and it became apparent that the property did not have listed building status. Fortunately sufficient research had by then been done to make out a case as a result of which listed building status was granted in 1980. It also became apparent that, since the end result would be multiple tenancy, the alterations to Nos. 5 and 6 had been subject to very strict fire regulations; such that all original internal features were destroyed or cased in appropriate fire-resistant materials, even including the ceiling joists. It was too late to make a photographic record of the status ante in this part of the property but it was possible to have access to No. 2 for this purpose before the developers started work again.

Unfortunately at this time two major disasters occurred in that the front door and window of the ground floor of No. 2 were reversed, to make more use of the available area, but destroying the symmetry of the entire frontage; the bottom two steps leading to the main door were extended to reach the front door of No. 2 and cased in concrete; and the bow window of the ground floor back room collapsed and was replaced by a flat sash window. This destroyed the mirror-image effect of the proportions of the back block.

At this time also, the entrance door to No. 3 in the communal passage was nailed up and the three light window in the back hall cut out thereby allowing an unbroken length of fire resistant board to be installed in the passage. The panel, edge to edge planking, round the window was covered with hardboard and the other 5 panels were similarly covered. When scaffolding was put up to re-front No. 2 the opportunity was taken to include No. 3: lath and plaster was removed, stud work renovated and modern materials used to create a longer lasting plaster surface. This treatment was also used on the West face of the back block. In 1988, in No. 3 only, the lead roof of the bay window had to be re-aligned and sealed during which work the date 1874 was discovered. In 1992 lead round the trap door to the catwalk between the roofs of the front and back blocks had to be similarly dealt with and some slates on the roof renewed. This uncovered hatches in the West roof of the front block and the East roof of the back block facing inwards to the catwalk: as, maybe, dormer window frames. In 1994 a large part of the bay window on each floor was rebuilt and it was realised that the vertical glazing bars in the ground floor were, most unusually, of triangular-section zinc. These last three repairs were carried out to the specifications required for a listed building in a conservation area. In 1993 No. 1 came on the market and was sold, for development as a single dwelling. It was possible to obtain access and make a photographic record of the property which had not been altered or modernised for many years, and retained a number of original features, very few of which the developer destroyed. The same was true for No. 4 which had passed through several owners all of whom were careful in the alterations they made and the last of whom allowed a few, selective, photographs to be taken.

During all these years a very few pieces of documentary evidence had come to light mainly as a result of the research into wider aspects of Maldon's history being carried out by Dr W J Petchey: an extract from the will of Dr Thomas Plume (1630-1704) from a copy of his will (1719) in the Plume Charity Trust Minute Book (I) "...I also give what remains of my personal estate in the Exchequer towards erecting a workhouse for the poor of Maldon and the neighbouring villages"; a copy of a bill for the finishing of the workhouse, from the same Minute Book, dated 4, Nov 1719, including the sum of £1. 17. 6d for the "raising dinner"; and a copy of the will of Thomas Welles, glover, leaving access to a well on one son's property to another son

(1606). Dr Petchey has identified this man as living in the (now) Welcome Sailor and owning tanneries on the corner of St Helen's Lane (now Cromwell Hill) and Fullbridge Street (now Market Hill). Other important evidence linking Dr Plume's workhouse to the Union workhouse was found when research on relevant and available documents in the Essex Record office began: Specifically, from the Minutes of the Board of Guardians (GMM 1A and 1-11) an entry for 27 Jan 1836 "...that arrangements be entered into for the purchase of the workhouse at Maldon for the use of the Union...". At the board meeting on 10 Feb 1836, the three (Maldon) parishes having assented, a valuation of £840 for the workhouse and premises and £550 for cottages and appurtenances was accepted and forwarded to the Poor Law Commissioners for approval. A Report of the Commissioners for enquiring into charities quotes Dr Plume's will and identifies the workhouse as having been built under the terms of the will and ...lately sold under the provisions of the Poor Law Amendment Act. This is the first explicit indication that the two foundations at Maldon were one and the same. The Tithe Map for 1838 completes the evidence that they were also the same buildings: it shows 3 contiguous areas, all numbered 419, on the North of the lane and West of the road (neither of these being actually named); these are all listed as Maldon Union and show various blocks of buildings in rather fuzzy outline; the main block is however quite clearly a representation of the present property.

Chapter 3
The Union Workhouse 1835 - 1875

The minutes of the Maldon Board of Guardians (1A and 1-11) cover the period 1835 - 1875 after which they continue but with reference to St. Peters. Under the terms of the Poor Law Amendment Act (1834) the Maldon Union was set up to cover the three Maldon parishes; St Peter's, All Saints and St Mary's, together with 29 other parishes extending along both banks of the Blackwater estuary. This increased greatly the potential number of paupers who according to the Act had to be sent "in" to the workhouse rather than receiving "out-door" relief. This problem was the first to be faced by the Board of Guardians when they met for the first time on 15 Dec 1835, when a plan for the enlarging of the workhouse prepared by Mr Sadd was produced and it was decided to set up a committee to examine ways of making the same "efficient for the purposes of the Union". On 24 Feb 1836 Mr Sadd produced a plan for raising the roof and various workmen were employed under his superintendance to carry out the work. This manoeuvre meant exactly that: winching up the rafters, heightening the walls, re-siting the rafters and replacing the roofing slates. It also explains the imposing aspect of the building and gives a firm date for the whole of the top floor of the main block.

Beside enlarging the workhouse the Board had to comply with the requirement in the Act that the sexes be separated and to this end had already, on 15 Jan 1836, authorised the removal of the "old staircase and partitions and the affixing of new ones". Once again various workmen were to be employed: Mr Samuel Cannon to complete the staircase on the Right entrance and Mr William Hayward that on the left, with others, "according to the plan and specification now produced" and under the superintendance of Mr Sadd. This provides, again, a firm date for the, wider, front staircases in Nos. 2 and 3. These created a total barrier between the Women's (South) side and the Men's (North) side: the women inmates being required to use the back door of No 1 and the men the back steps in No 4 or the staging. It must have been rapidly realized that this arrangement made the Master's or Matron's access to either side very complicated and time consuming so connecting doors had to be inserted at ground and middle floor level at the bottom of the staircases in No 3.

As a consequence of this, and other work, it was obviously apparent that major repairs were required to renovate the previous building: as, for instance, the kitchen chimney had to be pulled down and rebuilt; a stone floor laid in the room appropriated to the men and Mr Webber and Mr Cook, carpenters, were "to do the necessary work required in putting the several rooms in the workhouse into immediate repair" according to the plans and specifications of Mr Sadd furnished to them. This led to the uncovering of further problems such that Mr Sadd had to examine the cills in the room where the stone floor was to be put down and of such other parts as require immediate attention, which led to Mr Baxter being instructed to pull down and rebuild the chimney "at the Hall there, i.e. the said House" and on 9 Mar 1836 it was agreed to new board and plaster the rooms on the ground and first floor " ...and do such other work as is described in the specification this day delivered to the Board and marked A and signed ...". The following week Mr Sadd was authorised to have new windows made and the old ones were to be sold under the direction of the committee. This was a sub-committee established on that same day, any three to form a quorum, to deal with matters pertaining to the building works. From this time onward detailed minutes of alterations no longer appear, only general, mainly financial, matters coming before the Board for their consideration as, for instance, on 30 Mar 1836 Mr Sadd was given permission to continue with the works proposed by him and specified in the paper marked B and signed by the Chairman. Likewise, in May he was to proceed with the works as specified by him relative to the Master's House and Board room for which there is no mention of a specification at all.

During this time the able bodied men had been employed as casual labourers digging foundations for walls to separate the categories of inmates; 3 pumps with the necessary pipes had been purchased and installed and the new complex was insured with the Norwich Union for £1900. Norwich Union asked for a sketch or ground plan to be forwarded before accepting the application but, if this was indeed sent, it has not survived in their archive. Neither are there any plans at the Public Record Office and the various drawings and specifications presented to the Board by Mr Sadd were not traceable at the Essex Record Office. By the end of 1836 the workhouse was completed in so far as able bodied men and women, the sick and the infirm were all accommodated in separate sections of the main building.

This left the problem of housing children (age 7-15) separately. For this a new building was erected on the site over the period July - Oct 1838. This can be identified as a truncated T shape on the Tithe Map. Another problem was the question of sanitation: this took two years to solve but eventually, on 9 May 1839, Jno. Sadd and R. Cawston were paid the final balance for 2 water closets upstairs for the use of the sick poor and 2 in adjoining buildings. Each alteration was followed by its attendant problems: as for instance, in July 1839, the great gateway into the lane had to be paved and grates and drains made to take away the rain water to prevent it running into the school "... and to gravel the yards ..." which even as late as November 1839 did not provide separate exercise areas for all the categories. At this time also a porch was added to the East front of the main block.

By the time of the 1841 census the Union was listed as having 80 males and 96 females of whom 19 were boys and 14 girls under 10 years of age;

UNION WORKHOUSE
Artists' impression

1836 - 1875 only

together with the Master, his wife and son, and a Schoolmaster and Schoolmistress. After this the infrequent building references are mainly concerned with adjustments to meet the increasing number of Public Health requirements especially after 1842 when, in September, the minutes record the presence of cholera in the House. There appears to have been no great urgency over this, once the immediate scare had died down: a sub-committee was not appointed till 18 May 1848 and no decisions were taken till Nov 1848 when it was agreed that "...the room now used as a storeroom should be partitioned to such an extent that the infections ward for women should be formed of the length 22′ 6″ and width 16′ 8″ and the entrance made to it from the men's sleeping quarters ...". On 11 Jan 1849 a tender by Geo. Hearn for the erection of a leaden pump in the wash-house was accepted. The following week Sir John Walsham, Assistant Commissioner for Eastern England finally paid a visit, having been asked on 16 Mar 1848, and recommended that certain rooms should be ventilated as at Rochford, i. e. perforated louvres. Additional pumps and water closets had to be provided as the number of inmates increased and the well seems to have needed regular repair. In 1854 cholera struck again in the area but not, apparently, in the workhouse, from which it can be deduced that the alterations and arrangements made earlier were efficient.

Unfortunately, in 1864, there was a severe outbreak of small-pox: such that the school children had to be sent to a house on Cromwell Hill lately used as a school and the whole workhouse school building was given over to isolate the small-pox cases. This being another temporary expedient the Poor Law Commissioners sent a peremptory letter and on 16 April another sub-committee was formed to consider how to provide "proper accommodation" as instructed in the letter. By this time the site, with the building of an infants school in 1852, had virtually no room for custom built isolation wards and, this being reluctantly recognised, on 10 May 1864 it was agreed to take into consideration the propriety of either enlarging the present workhouse or erecting a new one. The reluctance to come to a decision led to delay after delay as various solutions were considered and discarded. As late as 17 May 1870 it was still hoped that the existing premises could be satisfactorily adapted and it was decided to appoint an architect and surveyor to inspect the workhouse to see if it could comply with the requirements of the Poor Law Board of Commissioners. As a result of this report on 14 June 1870 it was agreed, unanimously, that a new workhouse would be built. This time they did not renege and the construction of St Peters proceeded at such a pace that on 25 Mar 1873 notice was given that the Board of Guardians of the Maldon Union would give up possession of the present Union premises "...as at the 15th next ensuing..." i.e. 15 June 1873.

On 18 Sept 1873 it was decided that the workhouse (i.e. the old building) would be advertised for letting either as a whole or in part at about £400 p.a.

if whole; and that the rent be apportioned to each parish by a competent valuer. This arrangement does not appear to have been satisfactory since, after several meetings between the Overseers of the Poor of the three Maldon parishes and a committee for the Old Workhouse set up, ad hoc, by the Board of Guardians, it was arranged to sell by Auction at the Kings Head in 2 lots on 31 Aug 1875. Reserve prices were set at £800 for Lot 1 and £500 for Lot 2. On 18 Sep it was concluded that "...the seal of the Board be affixed to the conveyance of the Old Workhouse...to Messrs. Warren and Humphries ... and that the price of £1350 be paid ..."

The architect and surveyor appointed in 1870 was Mr Frederick Chancellor. The appearance of this name in the Guardian's Minutes led to the discovery of his deposited archive at Essex Record Office amongst which was an, unsuccessful, design for the new, St Peters, workhouse. Rolled up in this were the plans he drew of the old, Maldon Union, workhouse. These consisted of 3 sheets of cartridge paper, 41" x 21" in size, and delineated the lower ground level of the main block together with the ground plan of all the outbuildings; the front ground level of the main block with the upper floors of the outbuildings but the middle floor of the school; and the middle floor of the main block with the top floor of the school. The sheet outlining the top floor of the main block was absent: this would have been a very small drawing on the left hand side of a large sheet and, if separated from the other sheets, would have been unidentifiable for what it was except by someone very familiar with the building The plans are meticulously drawn to a scale of 1" to 10': and labelled very clearly except that the ink has faded and some words cannot now be read. There are a number of measurements of individual rooms and spaces including heights and changes in levels. Fenestration and doors are only shown as apertures, making interpretation difficult; fireplaces and water closets are indicated and even the number of beds in each sleeping room or hospital ward is pencilled in. It is possible that some labels could refer to projected alterations should the Guardians decide to adapt the old building but the overall impression is of an overcrowded site with no further space to build any more dedicated buildings e.g. a boiler house or an isolation block. It is, therefore, most likely that Chancellor's plans show the buildings and their usages as at 1870. This makes it possible to reconstruct its appearance at the time when it ceased to be a workhouse. In particular, the East aspect is confirmed as flat-fronted with a porch and porter's room masking the entrance; blind windows on the East of the North wing are occasioned by inserted fireplaces; the "coach" entrance on Market Hill is deducible and the wall down Union lane is only pierced by 3 openings: one at each end of the South range and another on the Western side of the Infants School.

Also in Bundle D/F8, redesignated D/B 629 A & B, were a number of earlier plans which identified the Infant's School as a two storey building; the plans of which were dated 1852. This plan, and elevation, was not signed but, according to the Minutes for 2 Nov 1852, (James) Beale, the Master, was to be paid £5 for drawing up plans and specifications for the new building. The other plans in the bundle are signed T. Bray and dated on a plain seal 1842. One labelled No. 2 (26″ x 18″) shows the three-floor main block using the East Front as ground level; the other labelled No. 1 (31″ x 25″) shows the proposed 2-storey South Range using the lower ground level as the base line. According to the Minutes it was, however, late 1848 before £465 for alterations was agreed and signed. Plan No. 2 was colour - coded but no key has survived; comparing these plans with those of Frederick Chancellor makes it possible to deduce and identify and date many of the features still in situ.

HILLSIDE, MARKET HILL
ARCHITECT'S PLAN
Main Block - Ground Floor

W

No scales given

origionals not to same scale

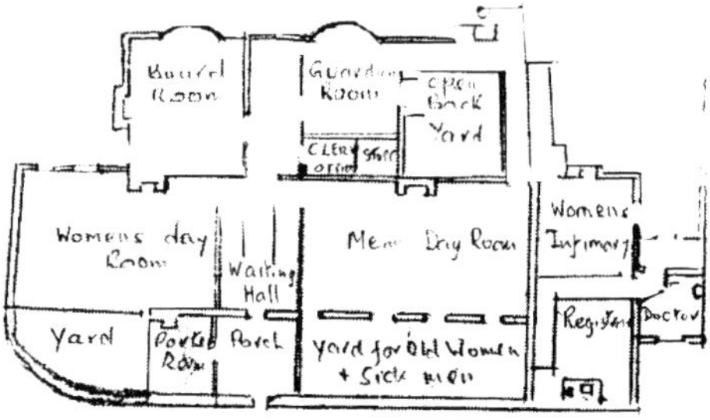

CHANCELLOR - 1870

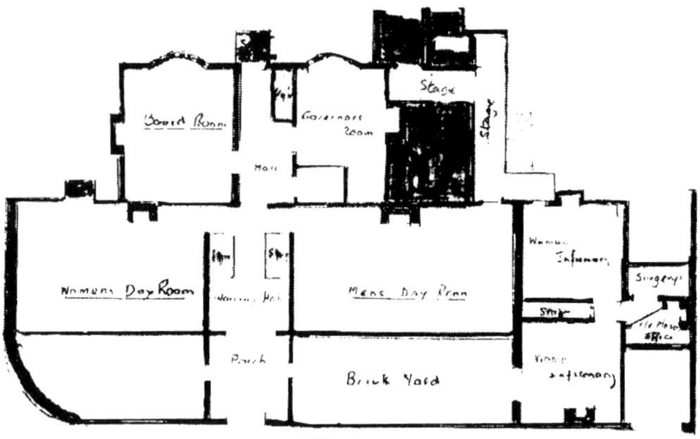

BRAY - 1842

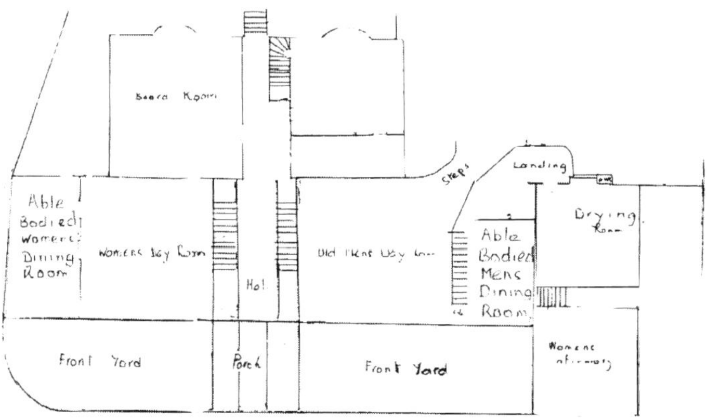

SADD - 1836

Chapter 4
The Core (Plume) Building

Rolled up in bundle 629A was one, last, sheet: a wash drawing on ordinary paper (26" x 21") not stamped by the Poor Law Commission nor otherwise dated, nor signed. It shows the East ground level and the West, lower ground level, on the same plane and has more the appearance of a working drawing than an architect's plan. The Guardians Minutes for 1835/36 make it clear that Mr Sadd produced at least five such drawings, the last two of which are noted as "marked A and signed" and "marked B and signed by the Chairman". The first, for "enlarging" the workhouse appears to have been sent to the Poor Law Commission and either not returned or not surviving as it would have a seal and/or date stamp. The other two were in connection with raising the roof and making new staircases. The drawing is manifestly not to do with raising the roof but has blue colour coded staircases indicating a new construction, from which it is a reasonable presumption that this is the specification and plan presented on 13 Jan 1836 and it was drawn up by Mr Sadd. Unfortunately the colour code key is absent and it is not possible to tell whether the labelling represents the then, or proposed, change of use. There is no fenestration, few room sizes, and not all fireplaces or doorways.

However, in conjunction with the Tithe Map (1838), this item is of paramount importance in providing glimpses of the earlier, parish property. The Sadd archive at the Essex Record Office contains disappointingly little: a Day Book itemizing 4 1/2 days labour for 12 Nov 1831 for cleaning away and digging foundations and making new privies, on the Maldon Workhouse Account. This is shown on the extreme Western boundary of the land as a five seater, presumably earth closets, on both Mr Sadd's plan and the Tithe Map. The School and a central block of outbuildings are shown on the Tithe Map but not on the Sadd drawing. The school was not agreed until May 1838 and as late as August 1837 Mr Sadd was to prepare estimates for altering cottages to be appropriated as schools, these cottages having been vacated in the previous March. These cottages, the central block on the Tithe Map, appear to have been almshouses attached to St Peters parish for which their Overseers of the Poor were paying rent until June 1837. This anomalous situation, viz.: that the later Tithe Map records buildings not apparent on Mr Sadd's plan arises from his expectation that the cottages would be demolished to free space for separate men's and women's exercise yards and a site for a school was not part of his brief as early as 1836. Both the map and the plan show a continuous North range of outbuildings and a small block half way down the Lane on the South side.

Documentary evidence for the earlier, parish, workhouse from other sources is very sparse. Other than the accounts found by Dr Petchey there are no further references in the Minute Books of the Plume Trustees since, once the

HILLSIDE, MARKET HILL
Outbuildings

W

Sadd
1836

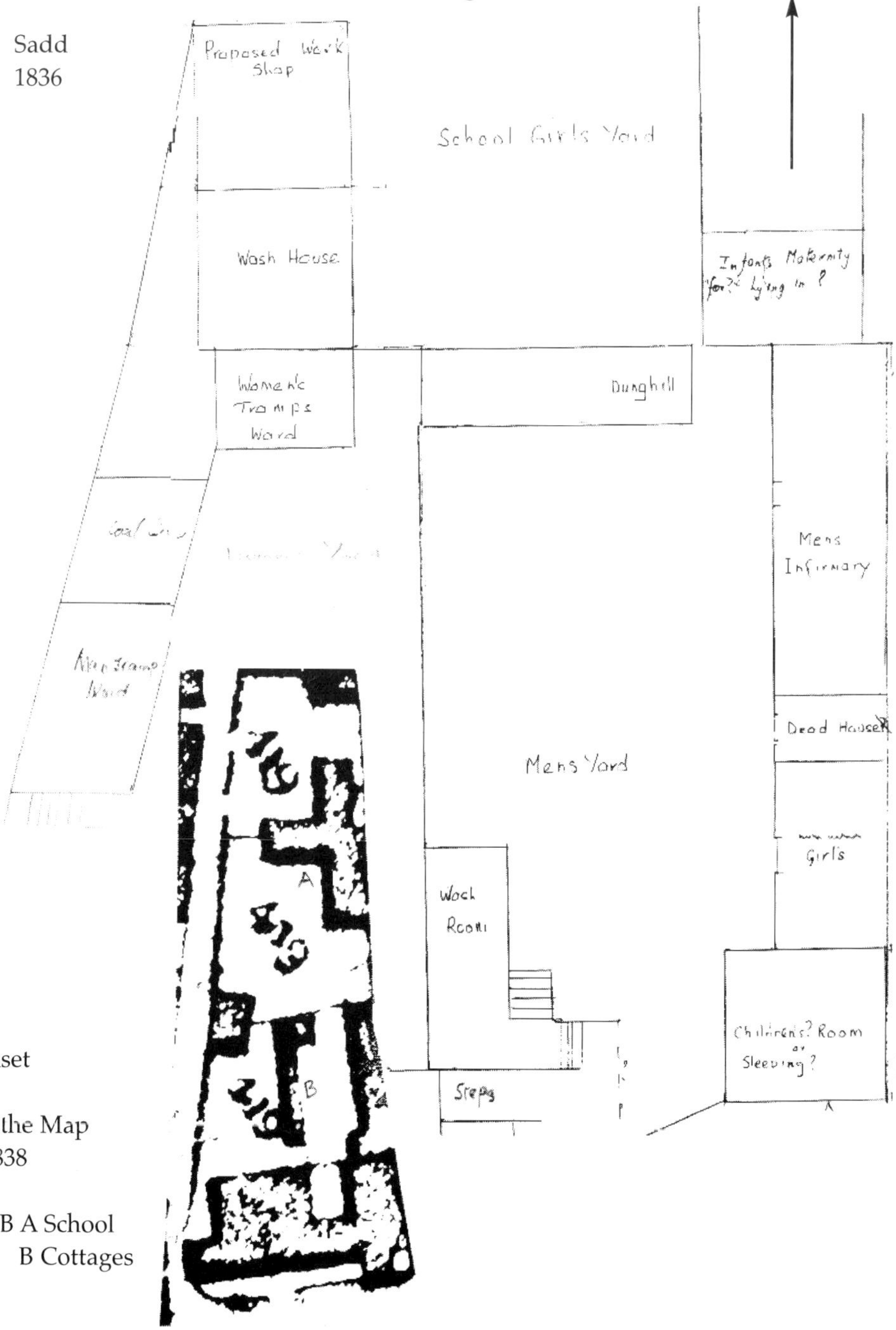

inset

Tithe Map
1838

NB A School
B Cottages

building was completed, they were not responsible for the running costs which devolved on the officers of the three parishes, particularly the church wardens and Overseers of the Poor. For the period immediately following the handing over of the property c1719 only the Churchwardens Accounts for All Saints with St Peters survive (1716-1754) (D/B 3/8/15A) at the Essex Record Office and nothing has been traced elsewhere. On 6 May 1726 there is an entry resolving "...to discharge Widow Shellock from ye care of ye wkhs ...Widow Hurrell be chosen governess for 1 yr paying her £6 ...". On 8 April 1729 Margt. Rawlins, widow, was appointed for $^1/_2$ yr at $2^1/_2$ gns. This begs the question as to whether Widow Hurrell served more than her initial year but makes it quite clear that the workhouse was being run more like an old-fashioned poor house than what Thomas Plume had envisaged by the use of the word "workhouse".

It took twenty years for this error of interpretation to be realized. On 16 November 1741 there is an entry in the same All Saints Rate Book indicating that at a general vestry meeting it was resolved "...to put the workhouse into repair in order for the employment of the poor..." "...and to provide a person proper to take care of and govern the workhouse ..." Twelve years later, in 1753, there is a further entry "... to treat with Mr Gibbons, the governor of Hatfield Workhouse about his undertaking that office for the Maldon Workhouse..." These two entries leave a number of interesting questions unanswered, and unanswerable, but make it quite clear that a major re-organization of the management of the workhouse took place at this time and more especially, since the position of governor would have been residential, that, at the very least, private domestic quarters would have had to be provided. This gives a date c1750 for the back, West, block leaving only the East front block to have been the original, core, structure.

It is consistent with the misinterpretation of the instruction to build a "work-house" that the local builders and craftsmen would be behind the times in method and design and that they would have built a late Stuart, East Anglian type rather than a Queen Anne, early Georgian, London design. This is crucially borne out by the photographs taken in the 1970's when the chimney in No. 2 was demolished revealing studwork with brick in-fill on the West wall followed by studwork with tile in-fill and a blocked-up window. On a mirror image basis this would give another blocked up window in No. 3, if not others in Nos. 1 and 4, thus confirming that this, West, wall of the front block, had been an outside wall. Nos. 1 and 4 have fully beamed ceilings and Nos. 1, 3 and 4 have heavy posts with grown knees, trennails and adzed marks set in a recognizable cill much broken up and cased in by later alterations. The bressumer, also much cut into and cased, is identifiable too. No. 4 has a blocked door leading in to No. 5 and a staircase down to lower ground level on the right of which, under the floor level, is at least one 2 ft. wide brick wall underpinning the downside of the hill level like a vault.

1741

At a General Vestry of the several Parishes of All Saints, & St. Peters in Maldon held this [illegible] Day of November 1741, It is agreed to empower the present Overseers together with the Churchwardens of the said several Parishes to put the Workhouse in to repair in order for the Employment of the Poor of the sd. several Parishes, and likewise to have the Brewing & Kitchen Furniture put into proper Repair for use. It is likewise agreed that the Furniture which is at present in the Workhouse be equally Divided between the sd. several Parishes, and what more necessary Furniture is wanting to be bought at the equal Expence & Charge of the said several Parishes, & it is further agreed that the present Overseers together wth. the Churchwardens do provide a Person proper to take Care of & govern the sd. Workhouse

Parishioners of All Sts.	Parishrs. of St. Peters
Jam. [illegible]	James Lowndes
Tho. Sooley	[illegible] Maldon
James Vaughan	Isaac Malden
John Bohannan	John May
James Hawkes	John Hawkes
Mark Cole	Jos Pattison
John Clayman	Jam. Beadle
Jn. Choate	Joseph Digby
J. [illegible]	
John [illegible]	

D/B3/8/15A

Plume Charities: Trustees' Minute Book(I)

Entries relating to the construction of a Workhouse.

Page 9 [Meeting of 19 August 1717]

Memorandum upon Mr James Plume his not answering the Order of three hundred pounds payable to Mr James Lawrence and sent him the said Mr J. Plume the 26th of November last, and upon the ` redelivery of the said Order to the Trustees a fresh Order was drawn up and signed by the Trustees as followeth, vizt

Mr James Plume, Maldon Aug. 19 1717

Bee pleased to pay to Mr James Ongham and Mr James Lawrence or either , their Order the summe of three hundred pounds and place it to account of us the underwritten Trustees of Dr Plumes Charities given to Maldon &c. Your humble servants

Daniel Horsmanden Abraham Bigos
Francis Thompson

Page 15 [Meeting of 4 April 1718]

Ordered that a Bill of two hundred pounds bee drawn upon the Executor Mr James Plume payable to Mr James Ongham & Mr James Lawrence for which they are accountable to the Trustees.

Page 19 [Meeting of 8 November 1718]

It is Ordered that a Bill of one hundred and eighty pounds be drawn upon James Plume Esqr Executor of Dr Plume, payable to Mr James Ongham and Mr James Lawrence, being the remainder due to them for the building the Workhouse.

And also a Bill of eighty four pounds for Workmanship and stuff for the Pallisadoe and other Fences, Bedsteds, Shelves and Tables, and Bricklayers' Work towards the finishing the Workhouse.

[Continued]

Pages 25 - 27

At a Meeting of the Trustees of Dr Plume's Charities given to Maldon, at the Grammar School November 4th 1719 .....

The several Parties having brought in their Bills for Work and Materials for the finishing the Workhouse as followeth, vizt

Imprimis

the Carpenter's Bill amounting to	£ 114 - 17 - 04
Mr Pond's Bill for Nails &c	32 - 15 - 05 $^{3}/_{4}$
The Making the Linnen for the Workhouse	4 - 09 - 10
the Bricklayer' s Bills	23 - 19 - 01
the Smith's Bill	10 - 06 - 04
the Limeburner's Bill	04 - 09 - 10
the Glazier and Plummer's Bill	05 - 13 - 03
Matting and Cordage for the Beds	04 - 10 - 00
Clay and Sand	02 - 10 - 00
Expences of the Trustees' Journey to Witham	
to view the Workhouse there	01 - 07 - 10
The Raising Dinner	01 - 17 - 06
Sum' Tot.	£ 206 - 16 - 05 $^{3}/_{4}$

Which several Particulars. amounting to the .sum of two hundred and .six pounds .sixteen .shillings and five pence three farthings Wee the Trustees here present do Agree that here be an Order sent to Mr James Plume the Executor for the payment of the said sum, in witness whereof Wee have set our hands the day and yeare abovewritten.

Peter Robinson
Jonas Maldon
Sam Pond
Alex Lindsey
Abra'm Bigos
Francis Thompson

Transcript kindly provided by Dr. W. Petchey

The other, crucial feature, not discovered till 1993, is the presence of dragon beams on the middle floor of No. 1. Bearing in mind that the roof was raised in 1836 this means that the previous roof was hipped at the South end. There are no such beams in No. 4 owing to the cross beaming and raftering of No. 5. These few details make it possible for an impression of the core building to be created.

The gradient of Market Hill, then called Fullbridge St, was the major problem to be overcome when construction began, especially as a double slope downwards to the North and West had to be counteracted. Another problem was the shape of the site which was strictly constrained by the Lane. This meant that, in order to build to the proportions then accepted, the whole building had to be set back from a notional building line so that a 17′ 6″ South elevation with right angles at the East and West corners did not encroach into the lane. A third problem was the lack of space to build a South Wing comparable to that on the North. To counteract the gradient a platform of brick boxes of increasing depth supported by cross walls on the deeper end had to be built. The hill itself would have been steeper three hundred years ago and Fullbridge St. more of a sunken lane as much as 2 ft. below the present road surface so that the Northernmost "box" providing footings for the North wing is 7 ft. deep. On these footings a six bay timber frame was raised consisting of 6 pairs of 15 ft. posts with knees and one, Southern, set with dragon beams to support the hipped roof at that end, the cross wing providing support at the Northern end. The raising dinner, similar to the modern "topping out" ceremony, took place in 1719 and cost £1 17s 6d. It celebrated the literal raising of the framework by pulleys and ropes and sheerlegs into marked or numbered positions on the ground cill. This item for the raising dinner is part of the expenses incurred in finishing the workhouse presented to the Trustees of Dr. Plume's Charities on 4 Nov 1719, the whole amounting to £200 6s $5^{3}/_{4}$d. to be forwarded to Mr. James Plume, executor, for payment. Unfortunately the previous entries, 19 Aug 1717, 4 April 1718 and 8 Nov 1718 do not provide details except the latter where a sum of £84 lists ... "Workmanship and stuff for the pallisadoes and other fences, Bedsteds (sic) Shelves and Tables and Bricklayers work towards finishing the workhouse..." but gives no names of craftsmen. They do, however, make it clear that Mr. James Ongham and Mr. James Lawrence were mainly responsible and that £680 was paid to them in instalments for the main building work. Together with the final bill this means that £964 6s $5^{3}/_{4}$d was spent in toto. For this a fully equipped house of two storeys with jetted upper floor and three storey wing was erected. It must be emphasized that the half timbered aspect as shown in the artists' impression was only seen during the construction as the Essex style was to limewash for extra weather proofing. The lime burner's bill for £4 9s 10d on the final bill adds stress to this point. Further details relating to the core building only become apparent when the alterations of c1750 are taken into consideration.

THE CORE (PLUME) BUILDING
Artists' impressions

Chapter 5
Georgian Alterations and Renovations

In addressing the problems of turning a poor house into a workhouse the double slope of the Hill and the angle of the Lane were, once again, constricting factors. Intending this time to build a more Georgian edifice, space had to be found on a narrowing site for the "cube" proportions required. A large area of top soil extending several yards down the Lane and at the rear of the existing building had to be dug out and retaining walls built. Another constraint was the ceiling height / floor level of the building in to which the new structure had to dovetail. This resulted in a maximum-sized, double-cube: 22′ x 22′ x 22′. Accepting the already existing chimney as one point at which to key in the outer walls and building Southwards these measurements did not correspond with the "bay" proportions of the old building so a post had to be inserted from which to extend the South wall of the new block. This new post was revealed by the demolition of the chimney in No. 2 in the 1970s and shows quite clearly on the archive photograph. Digging out the slope did not create level footings so the brick box foundations varied in height under No. 2 and No. 3. The upper floors were constructed of studwork with tile in fill. The tiles were most likely to have been re-used from the roof since both blocks were probably re-roofed with slates with a lead catwalk between them.

The West elevation of the new block was flat and plastered, with three windows in the upper floors and one on each side of a central door. This door was approached from lower ground level by steps with hand rails and had a hood and plain rectangular fanlight. On the North side of these steps was a window but on the South side, instead of a window, there was a door giving access to part of the cellar / basement under No. 2. The windows were sash but on the North and South walls, because of the basic ceiling height restriction, they were a, lower, 6-pane light and only a 3-pane upper light. On the West wall they were two 6-pane lights with no pelmet area between the casing and the ceiling. The graceful bow windows in the two ground floor rooms could not have been built as early as this: the peculiar dropped ceiling effect requires the ceiling to predate the window. The bow door providing present day access to the garden of No. 3 was not there, either, even as late as 1870 when Chancellor shows this area flat- fronted and occupied by the kitchen sink. Consequently the bow windows shown on the Bray plan must have been built as part of the work done by Mr. Sadd "...as specified by him this day relative to the Master's House and the Board Room..." on 5 May 1836. Further references to windows in the Guardians Minutes viz: on 30 Mar 1836 "... new windows prepared and the old ones sold ..." and 25 Aug 1836 "... Mr Joslin to paint and glaze the sash windows..." help determine that the poorhouse windows must have been casement, probably 3 light mullions sliding horizontally. Two new chimneys were built externally to the North and South

GEORGIAN RENOVATION
Artists' impression

Inventory of Household furniture & belonging to Allsaints & St Marys Parish at Maldon in the County of Essex taken the 21st July 1810 by Joel Myers Appraiser

Bed Rooms

4 Beds 4 Straw Mattresses and 2 Bolsters 1 Bed in a new Tick Mattrass 3 Beds & 1 Bolster 1 Bed on Brewers Bed & 1 Bed on Staples Bed in new Tick 4 Bolsters 3 of them have Wt covers 6 Coverlids 12 Blankets 2 Coverlids 1 nearly new 2 Coverlids Knotted 2 Coverlids 1 on Brewers Bed 2 Straw Beds & 2 Do 1 on Staples Bed 2 Do 1 on Brewers Bed 2 Sheets 1 on Brewers Bed 2 Do 3 Blankets on Brewers Bed 1 Bolster with case & 1 without 3 Blankets & Pillows on Staples Bed (new) 10 Stump Bedsteds 1 Feather Bed & 1 Bedsted 1 Bolster with case on Staples Bed

1 Chest (Drawers & Hutch 2 New Spinning Wheels 1 Do & 1 Second hand

from the committee Room

4 Walnut tree Chairs large Glass Lamp Square Table with a Drawer Hutch Stool Slate & Card Board Large Linen Chest

from Kitchen

8 Wooden Trenchers Buck 7 Do Do 2 Large Pewter Dishes & 1 Small 6 Tin Pint Mugs 4 Do 1/2 pint 4 & 1 Pint

4 Iron Candlesticks Brass Ladle, Tongs Beef fork Hanger & Cutting Knife large Copper Boyler and Copper Lid, Brass Kettle & Brass Lid, large Copper Warming pan nearly new large Copper Saucepan & Do lid, 2 large Brass covers & 1 Brass Warming pan lids 1 Large Stool & 5 Short Do

Pantry

Large Kneading Trough & Cover 12 Small wooden Bowls & 2 Do with handles 3 Earthen Dishes & 1 pan, 10 Wood Spoons & 2 ladles 2 Earthen Pots large wooden Bowl, Seive & 2 Old Bellows tops Copper Saucepan meat Stand & tin Strainer Pork Tub & lid

Second Pantry
all the Shelves round as fixed

Hall 1 Large Pail & 3 Small Do

2 Land Tables 4 Old Chairs a Trivet with Shifting Bar Range as fixed fender Poker Tongs
Strong Iron Sifter Square Table large Chest Box Iron & 2 Heaters large Tin Tea Kettle & Saucepan with cover 5 Spinning Wheels & one odd Wheel in Large Chest in the Committee room 4 Sheets, 1 good Sheet round Towel & a Cloth 5 Bolster cases & 1 Sheet,

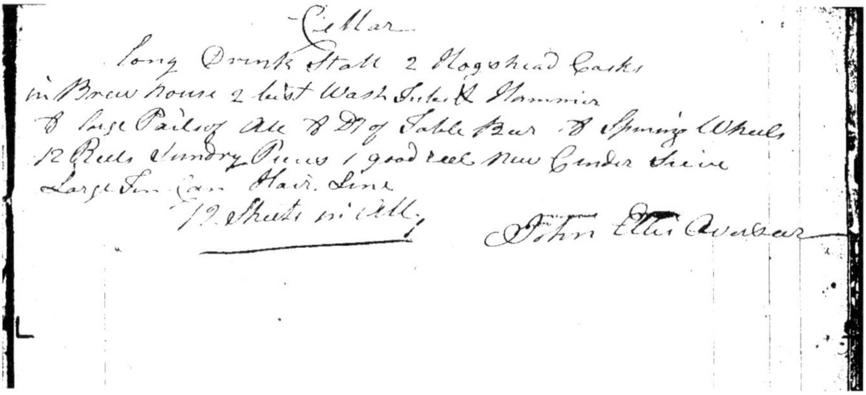
Cellar
Long Drink Stall 2 Hogshead Casks
in Brew house 2 best Wash Tubs & Hammer
8 large Pails of Ale 8 D° of Table Beer 8 Spinning Wheels
12 Reels Sundry Pieces 1 good reel New Cinder Sieve
Large Tin Can Hair Line
19 Sheets in All
John Ellis Walker

(E.R.O. D/B3/8/3)

HILLSIDE, MARKET HILL
Architects' plans

Upper Floors

W

No scales given

origionals not to same scale

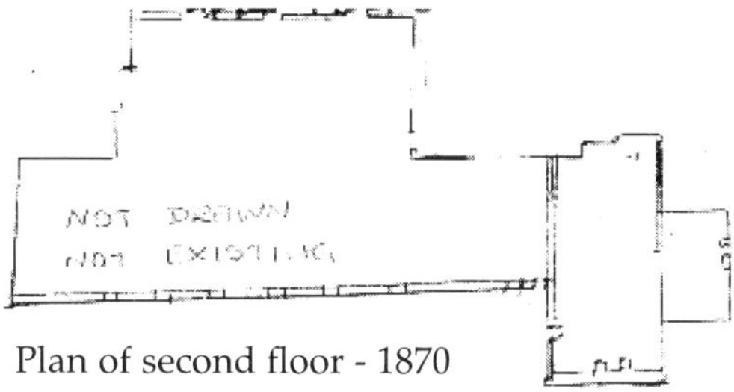

Plan of second floor - 1870

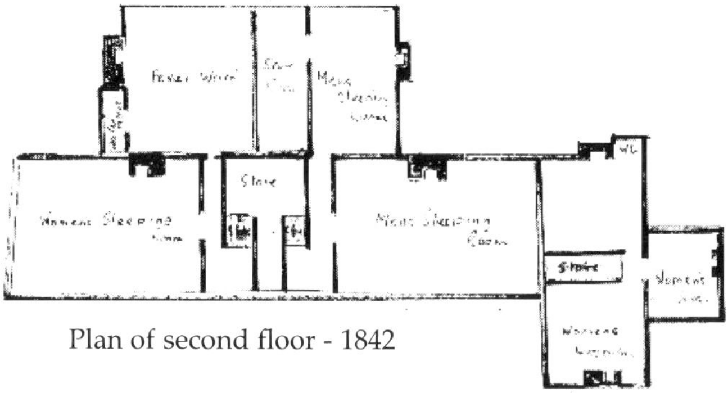

Plan of second floor - 1842

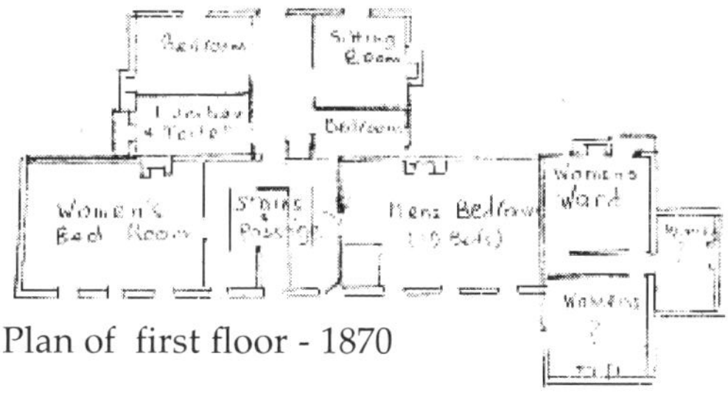

Plan of first floor - 1870

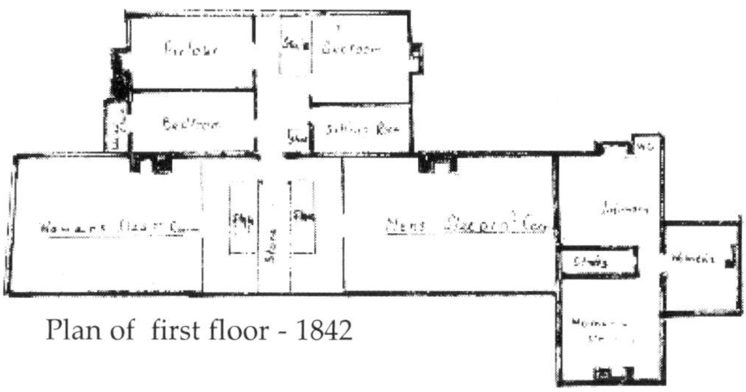

Plan of first floor - 1842

walls of the new block, one for the new basement kitchen and the room above and the other for the brewhouse and the rooms above. An internal chimney was built on a new South wall dividing the South end of the Hall into a smaller room and giving both sections a fireplace.

This additional block contained the Master's accommodation, as a flat / apartment, of four rooms on the first floor with a 3′ wide private staircase; two large rooms on the ground floor: one, self contained, for use as a fever ward and the other with storage space for use as an office for the Master and other officials connected with the administration of the workhouse with access to the private staircase; and the basement kitchen with two larders and a separate brewhouse with access only from the outside at lower ground level. The evidence for these functions can be inferred from an inventory dated 31 July 1810 (D/B 3/8/3) which lists furniture and fittings in a kitchen, pantry, second pantry and cellar / brewhouse. This was drawn up during one of the periodical quarrels between the officials of the three parishes. These quarrels arose because, at different times, one or other parish resented the amount of poor rate being levied and questioned the fairness of the distribution of resources... and threatened to leave. This inventory also makes clear that the main premises were known as the Hall which supports the interpretation that the first building was a Hall construction. Indeed as late as 24 Feb 1836 Mr William Baxter was instructed to pull down and rebuild "... the chimney at the Hall (i.e. the said house) ...". This was the Georgian chimney added to the North wall shown on Mr Sadd's plan and shown, resited on the West wall on both Bray and Chancellor and demolished in the 1970s revealing the clues to the previous structures.

By building the additional block the Hall had been freed from serving as a kitchen and the space could be utilized between meal times for the "employment of the poor" as required by the resolution of the vestry meeting of All Saints on 16 Nov 1741. Except for the mention in the inventory of 7 spinning wheels in various places it is not easy to discover exactly what work was provided. It was accepted that women inmates could do the domestic work: cleaning, cooking and laundering but there were continual arguments about employing the men to do jobs which, it was felt, should be available for those who were actively seeking to stay out of the workhouse. Unfortunately this admirable attitude conflicted with the purpose of a workhouse and more especially the requirement to keep costs down which could be achieved more easily by employing an inmate and paying a lower wage. The local tradesmen were also resentful that the workhouse was required to be self-sufficient, particularly after the Union arrangements were made and all unemployed had to go into the workhouse. This reduced their markets and caused friction right the way through but again, especially, after 1835 when many of the Board of Guardians were the self-same tradespeople.

It is possible that the North wing was not built until this, Georgian, alteration. Certainly the entrance door belongs to this period and the blocking of the door in No. 4 may have been done at this time. This could significantly alter the artists' impression of the core building since the roof would, in that case, have been one bay longer on the North end and hipped with dragon beam supports as in No. 1. There is no physical or archive evidence now available to allow a firm conclusion to be drawn. It is, however, possible to determine that at the same time as the West block was built the East core building was refronted. This is shown by the support post added to the Southwest corner down the Lane, into which was keyed a brick facing, under the overlap of the bressumer, which continues at the same height down the lane as the retaining wall. The frontage was re-done with laths on the existing studwork and hung as a curtain wall from the bressumer to the cill giving rise to the 4" gap behind the post in the W.C. of No. 3. The main door was made more imposing by a pilastered door case with hood on carved console brackets and iron railings up three steps. Three stone steps also led up to the yard, which was bricked, from the road level. Very plain, cosmetic, pilasters were also added to the Southeast corner of the frontage and the South front of the North wing.

The levelling of the Western part of the site provided more building land. This could be used for providing specialized areas for more of the functions of a true workhouse. A North range is shown on the Sadd plan, lower-ground level only, and on Chancellor as a two-storey block. In neither case is the labelling decipherable except the central room of a 30 ft. block is the Dead House. This means that no part of the South range was ever the "morgue" as supposed in 1948. Both plans show clearly the Eastern end as a short cross wing which corresponds to the building nicknamed the "granary" in 1948 and not demolished till the 1970s. Such wording as can be identified suggests hospital and infirmary use, specifically for men, by 1870. The South side on the Sadd plan shows a three room block with a set of steps, stone or wooden, which would have led up to the now isolated, hanging, door in the retaining wall to the lane. This block was completely superseded by the range shown on the Bray plan in 1842 and again the labelling is too faint to decipher accurately. No attempt seems to have been made to provide a Chapel; since the original foundation was based on the three Maldon parishes it appears that the paupers went to All Saints Church. One of the very few references is to the effect, in 1723, that the poor children in the workhouse were to sit in the North Chancel. Indeed it was 12 Dec 1839 before it was decided to appoint a chaplain to the Union. Other buildings to complete and close the Western edge of the site are shown on the Sadd plan but, in the absence of the colour code key it is not possible to determine whether they existed in 1836 or were proposed. The central block of cottages appear to have been built for St Peters parish paupers "...now in the Friary..." in 1802, probably for married couples and because of the quarrels between the parishes as to the treatment of differing classes of the poor. In 1818 the number of paupers in the workhouse were enumerated for the years 1813, 1814 and 1815, respectively, as 58, 54, 56 permanently "in" and 120, 117, 130 "occasional".

Both the Sadd and Chancellor plans show a single storey outbuilding running West from the Northwest corner of the back, Georgian, main block. This appears to have been a wash-house, i.e. laundry room, until the South range was built in 1848 and then to have been converted to a pump house, Mr Geo. Hearn's tender at £14 for the erection of a leaden pump in the wash-house being accepted on 11 Jan 1849. Staging is also shown on both plans running at first floor level with stairs to the ground level behind Nos. 4 and 5. The presence of the staging emphasizes the problems of a split-level site. The position of the access door to the kitchen, on the West side of the chimney-breast highlights another, very critical, problem. Bearing in mind that the West wall of the kitchen had a window and sink, this door, where the all paupers would have lined up to collect their meals to eat in their day rooms, was on the Men's side which was against the intention that the sexes should be strictly segregated. Chancellor's plan also shows the basement of No. 5 as a scullery - in which women paupers would have done all the washing up - but this, again, is on the Men's side and contravening the law. Likewise, when the porter's room was added to the porch in 1867, the old women lost their exercise yard and had to join the sick men who had to come through the building all the way from the North range men's hospital or right round the coach entrance and in again by the main gate. This possibility brings into focus a fundamental but intangible dilemma: namely, that having taken the original decision in 1835 to adapt the previous workhouse, it was impossible to re-locate the inmates to the back of the site away from Market Hill. However much the site was crammed with specific buildings, and however efficiently the law was obeyed, the building itself was an affront to polite society.

Chapter 6
Victorian Re-organisation

On 18 Sept 1873 the Maldon Express carried a news item under the heading "Maldon Old Union Workhouse - What is to be done with it?" This item and another on 2 Oct 1973 make it clear that the principal ratepayers of All Saints and St Peters and St Mary's were in favour of letting the building for some factory use at £150 - £200 per annum. This was less than the £400 the Board of Guardians thought to charge. Mr J. G. Sadd opined that a person hiring would be likely to expend £2,000 or £3000 about the building and the rent should be even lower at first! There appear to have been no applicants for the property to rent and the whole was sold on 31 Aug 1875. The various outbuildings were used over the course of time for factory and warehousing. The three-storey school was still there in the early 1930's when the ground floor was being used for seasonal pea-sorting; the laundry was still a laundry within living memory and the ground floor of the still existing part of the South range had trade signs for a plumber and a builder's merchant stacked against the wall in 1948.

According to David Hughes in his book The Maldonians part of the old workhouse was used as a granary as a temporary measure while the bridge was being re-built in 1877. This could have established a precedent from which folk memory continued to devolve.

The bulk of the £2-3000 Mr J. G. Sadd conjectured would be required must have been spent, probably by his firm and Maldon Ironworks, on adapting the main block vertically in to five tenements. Of these No. 5 being based on the North wing would have been the easiest requiring little alteration other than staging and steps to give it access at the back and a wall to the South East corner of the hospital ("granary") block to separate it from No. 4. Some work on Nos. 1-4 appears to have been carried out from 1873-75 while renting the building was under consideration since the lead roof of the large bay window of No. 3 is dated 1874. This means that the high boundary wall was demolished then, together with the porch and porter's room, and the iron railings inserted in the footings. The floorboards in the window area of the ground floor front room of No. 3 are not different from those in the main part of the room so the stone flag floor of the men's day room must have been taken up at this same time and the floor boards laid as a unit. The flags were re-used in the courtyard which had been brick.

Beside inserting the full-length, square bays in Nos. 2 and 3 more light had to be provided for Nos. 1 and 4, at least on the ground floor, so the four-light windows were inserted. Those in No. 4 are likely to be original since all the fenestration of No. 1 is out of keeping with the rest and the lights on all floors of No. 2 are also different. Individual house doors had to be provided - those in No. 1 and 4 replacing window apertures but those in Nos. 2 and 3 offset and

UNION WORKHOUSE, HILLSIDE

As sold August 1875

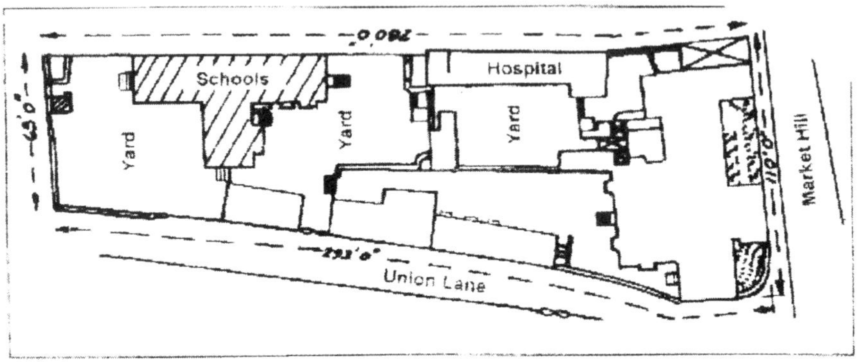

EAST FRONT

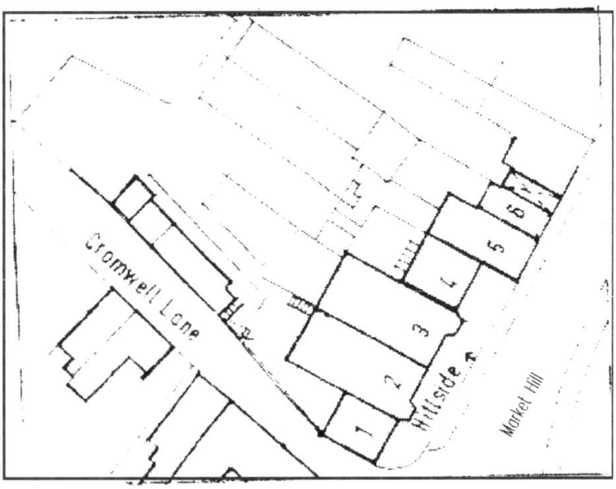

as divided - post 1873

displacing the ground floor casement windows giving rise to the anomaly in No. 3 that only the right hand half of the casement gives light to the ground floor room. Nos. 1 and 4 needed individual fireplaces, staircases and rear access. In No. 1 a chimney-breast had to be built internally on the South wall since it could not protrude into the lane; the Georgian party wall between No 1 and 2 was reconstructed and serves as part of the stair well. Unfortunately a steep 3' wide staircase running almost straight up from the, new, front door left no space to pass from the front room to the back. Given that open-plan living rooms were not acceptable in the late Victorian times, a curved wall, of dovetailed boards had to constructed and the front parlour became even smaller. A back door already existed with stone steps leading to lower ground level, the area noted on Bray's plan of 1842 as "...exercise yard for refractory women... ". Of the two WCs. built by Mr R Cawston in 1838 and shown on the Bray plan, the top floor one was incorporated into No. 1 and the middle floor one served No. 2. A staircase for No. 4 was created by taking 3' from No. 3 on both the middle and top floors; and fireplaces by utilizing the side of the main chimney-breast of the men's day room and similarly on each upper floor. The stone steps to lower ground level were boarded over and the existing staging re-routed to give access to the pump house and outbuildings which adjoined it and formed the boundary between No. 4 and 3. It is likely that for many years subsequently the WC for No. 4 was an outside "privy" in one of these outbuildings. On the other hand No. 5 had internal WCs on each floor these having been provided for the Women's Hospital and Infirmary in 1839.

The subdivision of Nos. 2 and 3 was facilitated by the two staircases built in 1836 already existing in the front ground-level range but the work required in the back, Georgian, part was more complicated. A partition wall had to be inserted on both the ground and middle floors. The partition was 4" x 4" posts with edge-to-edge planking rather than the tongued and grooved of 1836. The banisters on the Master's private staircase had to be removed to allow an unbroken length on the middle floor. On the top floor the door which had been inserted to enlarge the fever room in 1847 was nailed up. On the middle floor the door which had allowed the Master to pass from the men's side to the women's, and vice versa, was also nailed up. However the doors giving access to the centre passage from both the men's and women's side at the bottom of their respective staircases remained usable and the right of way for No. 3 was preserved. In the cellar / basement the two pantry doors were nailed up so that No. 2 could use the cellar underneath but only by going outside. No. 3 had the only internal access to the cellar. The doors leading to the men's yard on the North wall of the kitchen were bricked up, the Easternmost becoming a window with a sink under it. The sink marked on Chancellor's plan as occupying the Western bow window had to be removed completely to enable the centre window to be replaced by a door to give rear access for No. 3.

A major reconstruction, internally, was the realignment of the wall on the middle floor between the Master's sitting room and bedroom. This became curved, concave on the bedroom side to enable a small fireplace to be set aslant the main, back, chimney-breast and yet still allow an entrance to the sitting room, as it had been, at the very top of the back stairs. A lavatory was provided for No. 3 on the middle landing taking its water supply from the Market Hill side of the property. Water for the other tenements was routed from the back, pump house, supply. Gas was available at the back as the newer Union outbuildings, South range, North range and Schools had been supplied by Bryant and Co. as early as 1839.

Externally the outbuildings provided the North boundary between Nos. 3 and 4 except that the access door which the women had used to get to the kitchen, scullery and wash-house was bricked up. It is possible that not all these alterations were made simultaneously but only piecemeal as the letting arrangements for private use became clearer. It is, however, clear that architectural features in and around No. 3 Hillside can be accurately dated in four groups, viz.: c.1720; c.1750; c.1835 and c.1875 with a few even more specific.

HILLSIDE, MARKET HILL
East Front Nos 1 - 6 As altered 1874

ARCHITECTURAL FEATURES
NOTES ON PHOTOGRAPHIC PLATES

Capital letters in square brackets [ ] refer to Room usage plans in No. 3 HILLSIDE, ONLY

PLATE I CEILINGS

(a) No. 1: front block, middle floor, Southeast corner: Dragon Beam - giving support for roof of core building (1719) jetted on both South and East faces therefore: roof hipped - as it still is; cf. gable end on North Wing. Traces of similar beam are visible at Southwest corner.
(I am indebted to David Stenning for pointing out the importance of this feature)

(b) No. 1: front block, ground floor: fully beamed ceiling (1719); similar in No. 4; showing also chimney breast inset 1874 on South wall.

(c) [V] back block, lower ground-floor, Northwest corner: fully beamed ceiling (c.1750); showing also part of kitchen chimney breast and depth of outer, retaining, wall.

(d) [Q] back block, top floor, Southwest corner: coved, plaster ceiling with light-weight beams and iron bracket (1836).

PLATE II

(a) [M] front block, middle floor, West wall: post with grown knee and trennails giving support for original roof (1719). There are 5 further pairs of posts in all the whole block.

(b) No. 2: front block, ground and middle floor, West wall: octagonal pillar with iron collar, revealed by demolition of chimney breast, inserted to act as re-inforcement for addition of back block (c. 1750).

(c) [V] back block, lower ground floor: free-standing, load-bearing, octagonal wooden pillar on stone plinth.(c.1750)

(d) [C] front block, ground floor, West wall: post set in cill on brick footings (covered by skirting board), (1719); beam re-inforced at both ends by sawn timber and iron bolts and brackets when roof was raised (1836).

(e) No. 2: front block, ground floor, West wall: stud work with brick infill and blocked window. cf.(b) with tile infill. Much of the rest of the walling was (is) lath and plaster; the original plaster is mixed with horse hair.

PLATE III STAIRS

a) & (b [S] front block, middle floor: tongued and grooved stairwell (1836) newel posts and handrails and banisters re-used. See page 22 which shows, on Sadd plan, staircase in Old Men's Day room and pre-supposes similar for Women (or both) demolished by erecting one for each side in 1836. Comparison with newel styles in back block gives date c.1750 for (b) and 1719 for (a). Handrail (a): cut and dove tailed to fit; has no slots for tops of banisters. Handrail (b): iron piping covered with corded whipping twine to give better purchase for public staircase.

(c) [L] front block, top floor: all 1836

No. 3 HILLSIDE, MARKET HILL
Room Usage

1870
P - $^{2}/_{3}$ Mens sleeping Room
R+ Q - Fever Room

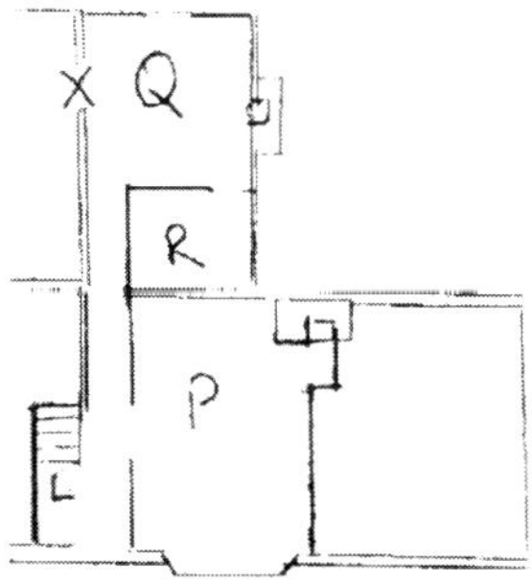

1995

X - Blocked Doors
P - Top Bedroom
R - Flat Kitchen
Q - Flat Bed-sit
L - Top front stairs
and landing

SECOND (TOP) FLOOR

J - Master's Bedroom
K - Master's Sitting Roomb
M - $^{2}/_{3}$ Men's sleeping Room
N - Not there

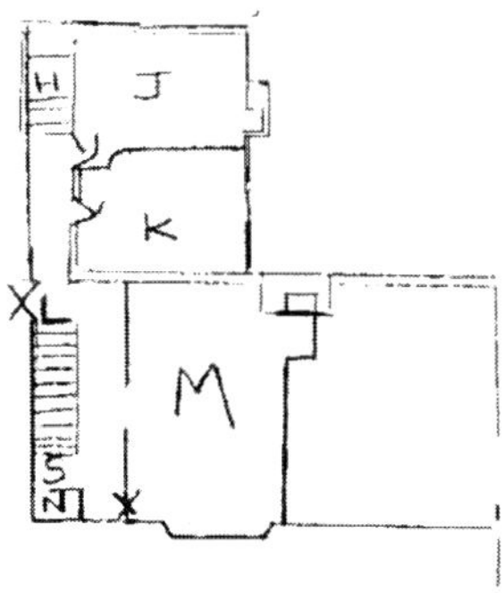

H - Back stairs
J - Back Bedroom
K - Bathroom
L - Top front stairs
M - Front Bedroom
N - W.C.
S - front stairs
and landing

FIRST (MIDDLE) FLOOR

No. 3 HILLSIDE, MARKET HILL
Room Usage

1870
H - Punishment cell?
V - Kitchen

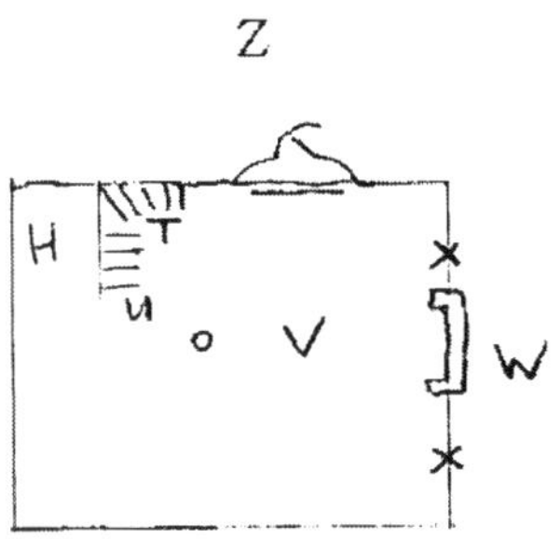

1995
X - Blocked Doors
T - Cellar Stairs
V - Workshop
W - garage
Z - Garden

LOWER GROUND FLOOR

A - not there
+
B
C - $^2/_3$ Men's Dayroom
D - $^1/_2$ Back Hall
E - Secretary's office
F - Store
G - Govenor's Room

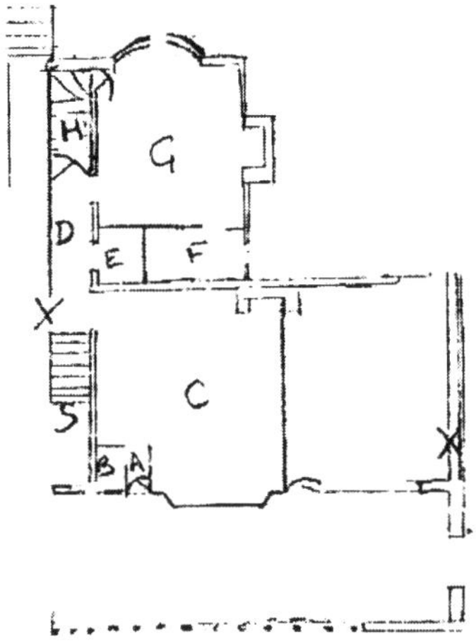

A - Lobby
B - W.C.
C - Sitting Room
D - Back Hall
E - Office
F - Kitchen
G - Living Room
H - Back Stairs

GROUND FLOOR

ARCHITECTURAL FEATURES
NOTES ON PHOTOGRAPHIC PLATES

Capital letters in square brackets [ ] refer to Room usage plans in No. 3 HILLSIDE, ONLY

PLATE III STAIRS (Con'd)	(d) & (c)	[T] back block: two views of stairs to workhouse kitchen(c.1750). Note narrower, private width; iron pipe hand rail (without corded whipping) and bars giving light to punishment cell.
PLATE IV EXTERNAL DOORS	(a)	Front block, ground floor, East facing: centre passage door, top step and hand rail (c.1750) hidden by porch (1836 - 1874); lower two steps cased in concrete (1980s).
	(b)	close-up of pediment showing flat tablature and ornamental console.
	(c)	[A] front block, ground floor, East facing: 3rd (of 4) individual doors inserted into brick footings and cill using window aperture as basis and transposing window to the left. (see plate VIII). all 1874 except threshold step: re-used section of cill. Some panes of glass and letterbox are modern.
	(d)	Back block, ground floor, West facing: centre passage door with steps and hand rails leading to lower ground level - all c.1750 except modern reeded glass upper panels.
PLATE V INTERNAL DOORS	(a) & (b)	[C] front block, ground floor, Southwest corner: double thickness door with original ironwork fittings (1719) resited in frame cut round 1719 post in 1836; showing also two steps into room necessitated when floor was lowered to restore headroom when beam (see plate II) was re-inforced; shows also cill; and brick footings covered by skirting board.
	(c) & (d)	[K] back block, middle floor: 4 - panel door, original (c.1750) furniture except hook and eye latch.
	(e) & f	[P] front block, top floor: vertical tongue and grooved with lighter bar strapping (1836) except for three modern repro. hooks.
PLATE VI WINDOWS & EXTERNAL	(a) & (b)	front and back block, West facing: top floor, both sash and casement (1836); middle floor (c.1750) replaced 1836; sash windows sold; ground floor bow window (1836); door: (see Plate IV); ground and lower ground on South side both modern: N.B. line of ground floor shows clearly either side of patio doors; and level of lower ground floor.

ARCHITECTURAL FEATURES
NOTES ON PHOTOGRAPHIC PLATES

Capital letters in square brackets [ ] refer to Room usage plans in No. 3 HILLSIDE, ONLY

PLATE VI WINDOWS (cont'd

(c) [G] and [V] back block, West wall: bow window (1836) - on 4" x 4" wooden posts with flat front and sash window (No. 2 had similar until 1980s); brick and plaster wall with door and two lights inserted 1874 to give No. 3 access to yard and garden area.

(d) & (e) front block No. 1, West facing i.e. back wall of core building: external and internal view of original window with heavy wooden mullion and 2 lights - could have been 3-light now partially hidden by weather-boarded wall of 'flying' extension for W.C.s installed 1839 (See plate IX for another view).

PLATE VII WINDOWS INTERNAL

(a) [G] back block, West facing, ground floor: bow window - 1836- showing fine quality carpentry provided for Master's office and similar in Guardians' Board Room in No. 2; see also Plate VIII(b).

(b) [V] back block, West facing, lower-ground floor: door and steps inserted 1874; previously a flat window with sink underneath. N.B. poor quality of door and depth of outer retaining wall

(c) No. 2. Back block, South facing, lower ground floor: half window below ground level giving light and ventilation to half-height cellar (c.1750).

(d) [L] front block, top floor, in ceiling outside door to Men's Dormitory: sash cord coming down from roof space to enable Master to control opening of louvres vents and 'trap doors' in said dormitory for extra ventilation.

(e) [Q] back block, top floor: 'trap door' and plate with hole for sash cord allowing louvre vents to be closed from inside the room. There are two similar 'trap doors' in the mens' dormitory and in the womens' side. This system was provided in 1848.

PLATE VIII ANOMALIES

(a) [H] back block: staircase well newel post and handrail (c.1750) showing holes for banisters on left hand side: removed when partition wall erected to separate Nos.s 2 and 3 (1874).

(b) [G] back block, West wall showing beam (c.1750) and 14" higher window frame (1836).

ARCHITECTURAL FEATURES
NOTES ON PHOTOGRAPHIC PLATES

Capital letters in square brackets [ ] refer to Room usage plans in No. 3 HILLSIDE, ONLY

PLATE VIII ANOMALIES (cond'd)

(c) [C] front block, East wall, showing post (1719) with half window cut behind it (1874) (See PLATE IV c)

(d) [H] back block (c.1750) looking towards staircase to top floor (1836) - note difference in width: right hand partition wall (1874) shows 4" x 4" posts and raised planks giving mock stud work effect. Note especially closeness of first door frame to top stair and newel post.

(e) [J] corner with door which cannot be resited to the right because of stairwell but.

(f) [K] fireplace required can only be positioned across corner of chimney breast in [J]: hence curved wall (1874).

PLATE IX ANOMALIES

(a) [C] Northwest corner: off centre fireplace (1874) on $^{2}/_{3}$rds chimney breast (1719) with shoddy cupboard to fill older hearth, and partition wall between Nos. 3 and 4 (1874).

(b) [M] Northwest corner: $^{2}/_{3}$rds of chimney breast (line of fire place can be seen in wallpaper) partition wall and stairwell of No. 4 creating alcove (1874). Shows also post, beam and floor boards (1719)

(c) [V] North Wall: chimney breast (c.1750 rebuilt 1836), left-hand side copper probably c.1750 right hand side range 1836 or 1874.

(d) No. 1. Internal view of mullioned window plus post and knee (1719)

PLATE X BLOCKED DOORS

(a) No. 4. Ground floor front, North Wall: door, with threshold, leading to North Wing (1719) before external door provided (c.1750).

(b) [M] middle floor front SE corner: door to porter's cubicle in Mens' Dormitory; not blocked till 1987: also shows 'skirting' board supporting heavy planked partition (painted to resemble beams) resited when stair well built (1836).

(c) No. 1 and cottage; South wall down Cromwell Lane: 'hanging door' in retaining wall; both built (c.1750) when land excavated to accommodate back block. There are traces of staging and wooden steps - but no traces of iron spikes on the top of the wall.

(d) [V] Southwest corner: door to pantry; nailed up 1874, bricked-up 1980.

ARCHITECTURAL FEATURES
NOTES ON PHOTOGRAPHIC PLATES

Capital letters in square brackets [ ] refer to Room usage plans in No. 3 HILLSIDE, ONLY

PLATE X BLOCKED DOORS (con'd)

(e) [Q]. Back block, top floor: door inserted in 1848 linking part of Men's Dormitory to walk-in storeroom and enlarging Fever Room.

PLATE XI WOOD WORK

(a) [L] adze marks; also on beam in [M]

(b) [M] Lambs tails.

(c) [M] Trennails.

(d) [M] contrast between broad (1719) floorboards and narrower (1874) in bay window - note even narrower 'filler'.

PLATE XII OVERVIEWS

(a) [L] looking SW from [M] stairwell cut into 1719 floorboards in 1836; double newel posts, lower handrail and banisters (c.1750) - resited; showing also partition wall inserted between Nos. 2 and 3 (1874); iron hinge of old-style door can just be identified: this door was an after(1836) thought cut in to enable the Master to pass from the Women's side to the Men's side instead of going all the way to the ground floor and back up again because at that time his private door was over the central passage and the, then, solid wall was part of his, private, W.C.

(b) [D] looking West through door frame (never any door) cut (1874) into back wall of front block (core building.1719) showing edge to edge partition wall with beamed effect erected to divide No. 2 from No. 3 on the left together with entrance door from central passage - nailed up - 1980s. At the end on the right in the hallway: door to kitchen steps, door to Master's office and door to Secretary to the Board's (stationery) cupboard - all c.1750; half board and plaster (1836); cow-bell, connected to bell pull on front door (1874) and still in working order. Near right: tongued and grooved planking for stairwell (1836) with door (1719) set in door frame cut into 1719 post in 1836. See Plate V.

(c) [V] to South of stairwell and under central, communal passage: narrow cubicle (cell) with wooden ventilation bars - for punishment of drunk and disorderly inmates?

WORKING DIAGRAM

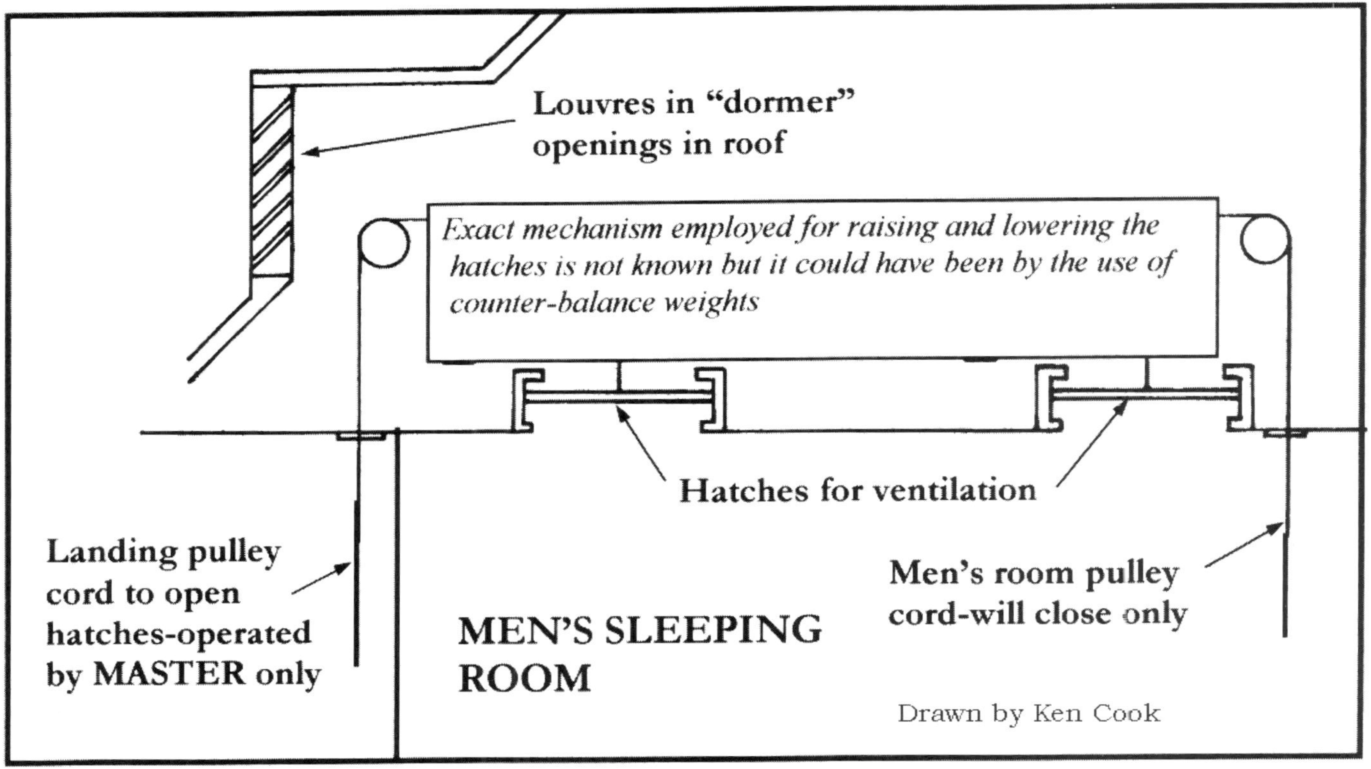

See Plate VII (d) and (e)

PLATE I

(a)

(c)

(b)

(d)

PLATE II

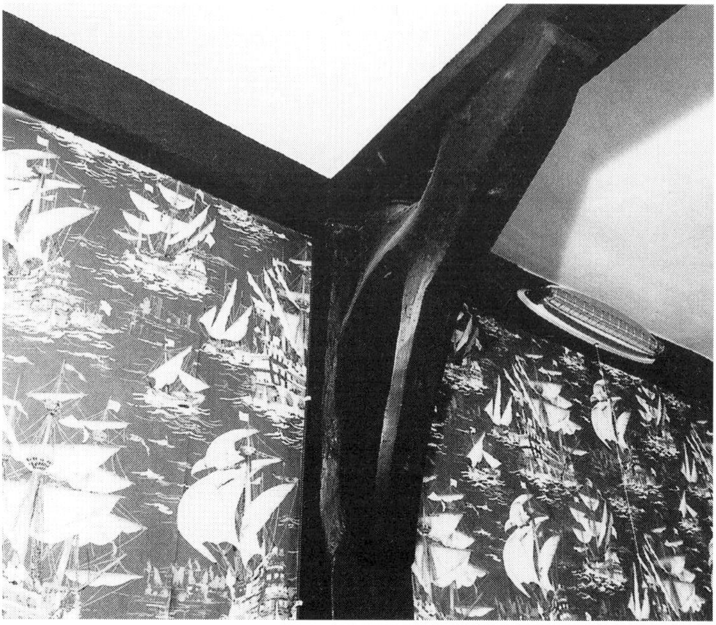

(a)

(c)

(d)

(b)

(e)

PLATE III

(a) (b)

(c)

(d)

(e)

PLATE IV

(a)

(c)

(b)

(d)

PLATE V

(a)

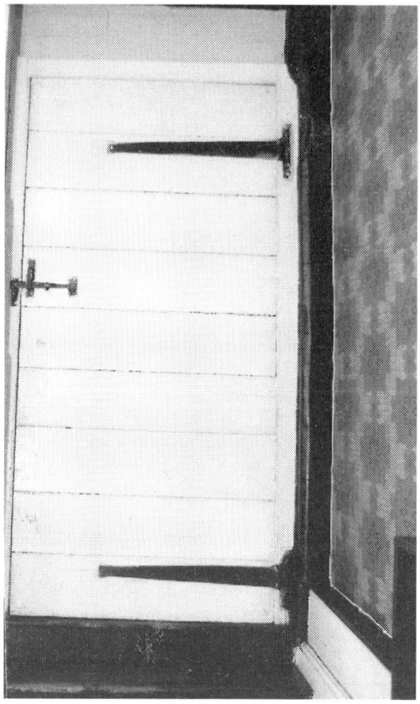

(b)

(c)

(d)

(e)

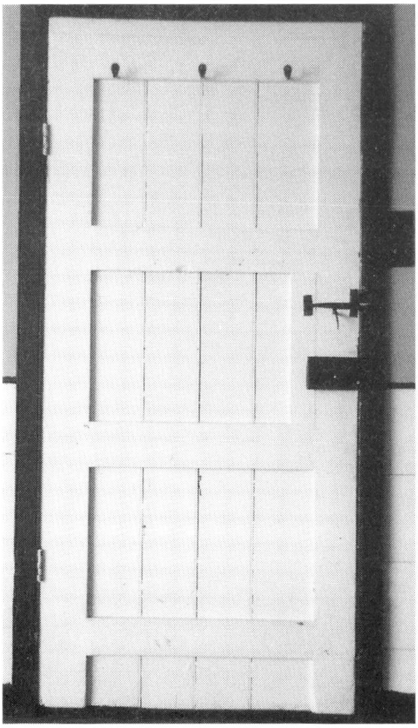

(f)

PLATE VI

(a)

(c)

(b)

(d)

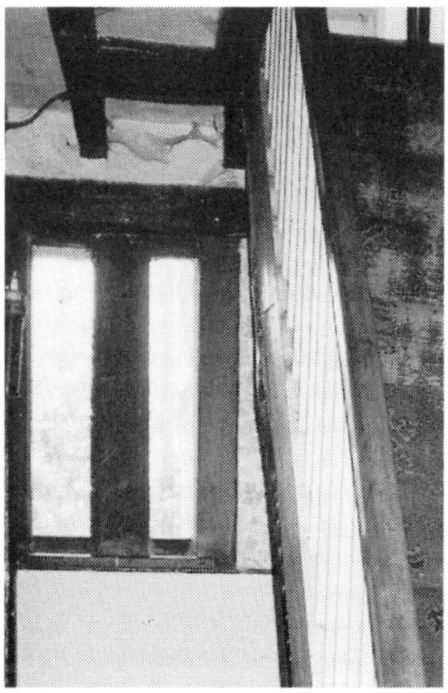

(e)

PLATE VII

(a)

(b)

(c)

(d)

(e)

PLATE VIII

(a)

(b)

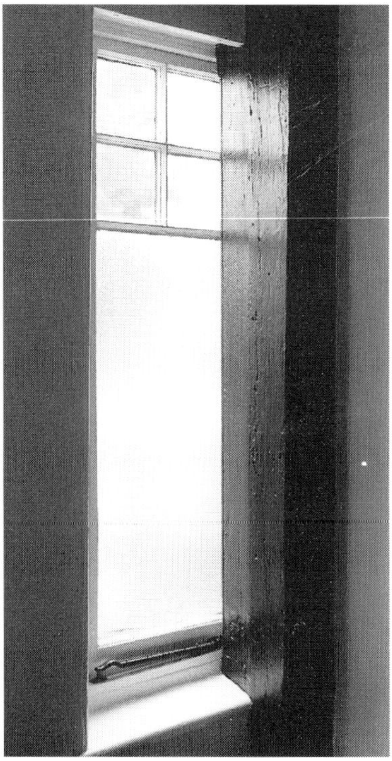

(c)

(d)

(e)

(f)

PLATE IX

(a)

(b)

(c)

(d)

PLATE X

(a)

(c)

(b)

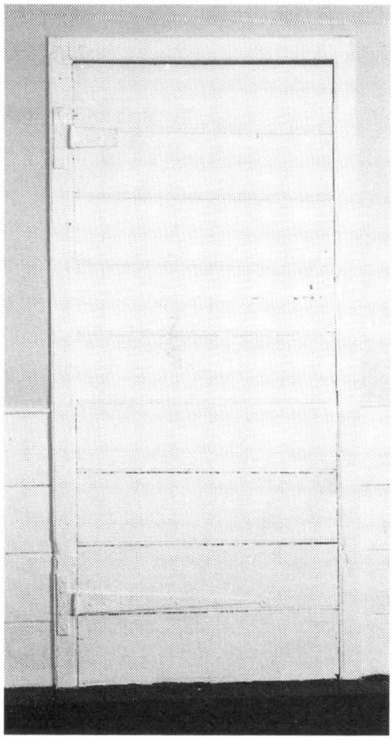

(e)

(d)

PLATE XI

(a)

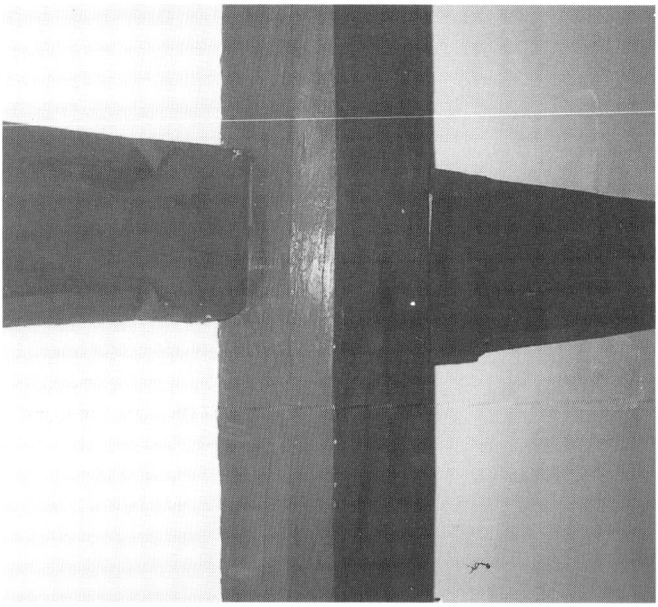

(b)

(c)

(d)

PLATE XII

(a)

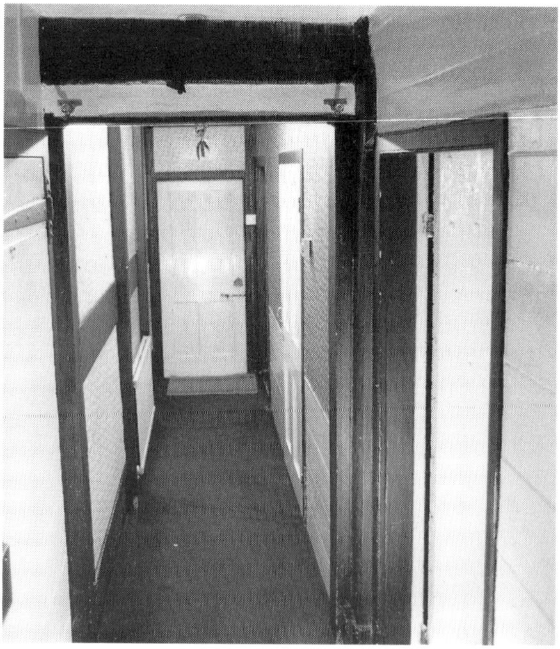

(b)

(c)